Ten Tasks of Change

Demystifying Changing Organizations

Jeff Evans and Chuck Schaefer

JOSSEY-BASS/PFEIFFER
A Wiley Company
San Francisco

Copyright © 2001 by Jossey-Bass/Pfeiffer
Jossey-Bass/Pfeiffer is a registered trademark of Jossey-Bass Inc., A Wiley Company.
ISBN: 0-7879-5345-8

Library of Congress Cataloging-in-Publication Data

Evans, Jeff, Ph. D.
  Ten tasks of change : demystifying changing organizations /
Jeff Evans, Chuck Schaefer.
      p. cm.
Includes bibliographical references and index.
    ISBN 0-7879-5345-8 (acid-free, recycled stock)
  1. Organizational change—Handbooks, manuals, etc.   I. Title:
10 tasks of change.   II. Schaefer, Chuck.   III. Title.
  HD58.8 .E94 2001
  658.4'06—dc21

                                    00-012104

Printed in the United States of America

Published by

JOSSEY-BASS/PFEIFFER
A Wiley Company
350 Sansome Street, 5th Floor
San Francisco, CA 94104-1342
415.433.1740; Fax 415.433.0499
800.274.4434; Fax 800.569.0443

www.pfeiffer.com

Acquiring Editor: Matthew Holt
Director of Development: Kathleen Dolan Davies
Developmental Editor: Susan Rachmeler
Editor: Rebecca Taff
Senior Production Editor: Dawn Kilgore
Manufacturing Supervisor: Becky Carreño

Printing 10   9   8   7   6   5   4   3   2   1

This book is printed on acid-free, recycled stock that meets or exceeds the
minimum GPO and EPA requirements for recycled paper.

Contents

Figures and Exhibits

Figures

Exhibits

Preface

Explosive growth in new markets, incredibly short product life cycles, and shifting global economies are creating an environment of permanent flux. The days of predictability and stability in organizations are essentially gone. Gone too are the methods of establishing and institutionalizing systems that match that environment. Today's organizations are responding with a new capability for intentional and rapid change. Agility has become a defining characteristic of successful, high-performing organizations. For today's environment, the ability to work at change must be institutionalized.

This book has been created to be a bridge between theory and practice in guiding organization change. The book links a rather difficult theory base to a basic organizational capability: planning and managing work. It approaches organization change as work, something that people can *do*, rather than as something that *happens* to them. This book provides a logical framework for thinking through the objectives of the change, planning the activities to achieve those objectives, and some "best practice" principles for their accomplishment. This book is a kind of catalogue of tasks and principles from which to pick and choose what to emphasize formally and when to let nature take its course.

This book has, as its underpinnings, a strong systems focus, an intention to enable and strengthen organizational learning, and a position of honoring individual choice, allowing people to be fully contributing members of organizational change.

One can approach change logically, but the work of changing organizations is not linear. You will get a better feel for this in Chapter One, which presents material about developing an appreciation for the state of your organization and the need for change. Because writing things down forces a linear representation of the work of change, we recommend that you first read the book from cover to cover quickly, as you would read a novel. Get the gist of the whole; then go back and dig into its meaning as you move bit by bit through your change process. Approaching the book this way will magnify your own creativity in the change situation, and that is important.

The methods in this book have been developed from a long practice in the field. They have been proven effective in a number of different organizational types and settings. They are based on a whole systems approach of jointly optimizing the business, processes, and people systems. This book provides managers and change practitioners with a model and an approach for dealing with change.

Approach

We practice participative approaches to organization change. Our approach is influenced by sociotechnical systems and includes large-group methodologies. Our beliefs about organization change are founded on a perspective that sees groups of people, and therefore organizations, as goal-seeking and intentional. Thus, our approach is sensitive to choice in the organization, honors what is often called "resistance," and allows for self-organization and rapid growth. This approach liberates the organization's innate capacity for rapid and intentional change.

The work of change often appears to be difficult and mystical to leaders faced with a change effort. Theoretical approaches often appear vague and overwhelming and tend to do little to guide action. Other approaches tend to be so detailed that they leave little room for adjustment or for understanding the dynamic that is occurring inside of complex systems.

The authors have developed the Ten Tasks of Change to enable participants in the change process to see the entire system. It is a directional framework that, more importantly, creates a bridge between theoretical models and mechanical processes. This approach looks at change as work—as something that people do. Framing this as a task provides a statement of intention that guides action in the system. This model also allows much more freedom and flexibility in the change effort and increases participants' contributions and satisfaction with the effort. Positioned within the context of work, the approach allows organizations to utilize existing competencies of planning work and working plans.

Audience for the Book

This book is written for the people we have begun calling "stewards of change." The phrase emerged from a discussion we had with a client about Peter Block's (1993) book, *Stewardship*. We have adopted the phrase in part because of the semantic confusions and overlaps that have evolved around the meaning of such terms as "change agents," "change leaders," "change managers," "opinion leaders," and so forth. (We'll talk more about the players in a change situation in Chapter Three.) We have also adopted the term as an invitation for actors in a change situation to think about themselves and what they do in a richer sense, illustrated by Block's subtitle: *Choosing Service over Self-Interest*.

Whether by personal choice or by assigned formal responsibility, change stewards work to guide others through the canyons, across the bridges, and around the trip points of a change journey. As change stewards, they will:

- Pay the most attention to the change, strategically and tactically

- Make sure that the key issues are surfaced and addressed

- Be sure that the right people are engaged and working productively

- Identify opportunities and capitalize on support

- Identify barriers and turn them into opportunities

- Be sure the change approaches are driving the right behaviors at all levels of the organization

- Dive into the details without losing their perspective of the overall process

- Make sure the leaders and targets of the changes communicate, communicate, communicate

Readers of this book might be executives or managers whose organizations are faced with the need to adapt. These readers, particularly if they have limited experience in guiding significant change, can find some very useful insights. Or the readers might be experienced professionals in the field of organization planning, development, and change. These readers will probably not find much that is startlingly new, because the propositions represented have evolved over years of practice and interaction with other professionals in the field. However, they may find new ways to frame the familiar, new insights into the challenges they face, or new ideas that they can build on and apply in their own practice. And finally, the readers may be targets of a change who want to do whatever they can to help make sure the right things happen for themselves, for their colleagues in the organization, and for the business they depend on. Unlike the executives, managers, and practitioners, these readers may not have a formal role or the formal authority for leading the change. However, they can find some very useful insights that will help them play a significant informal leadership role in the process.

How the Book Was Developed

This book is based on our collective experience and study in the field of organization design, development, and change, which reaches back to the formative days of organization development practice and open sociotechnical systems thinking (Emery, 1969; Emery & Trist, 1973, 1978). It presents a framework for compiling and sorting our experience into what we have called "The Ten Tasks of Changing Organization" and a set of beliefs about people and change that guide us in the application of what we have learned over time. It is an attempt to represent the multidimensional reality of our learning in the two-dimensional medium of the written word.

Our own notions about what has been happening in our practice primarily shape the models and propositions you will read here. However, few thoughts are truly unique to any of us. Ideas you will encounter in this book may seem familiar because they exist in the general body of knowledge in the field. Where our perspectives have been shaped heavily by the thinking of specific people, we make reference so you can go directly to the source and benefit from that wisdom also.

Summary of Contents

This book is framed around the ten tasks. The chapters correspond to the individual tasks and present an outline of the work required in each.

Chapter Zero provides the overview and approach that we have found to enable large-scale participative change. Change starts with an individual, and the individual must begin by becoming clear about the work required to change an organization.

Chapter One focuses on the first task—appreciating the situation. It outlines the areas required to create a business case for change and the corresponding dialogue to ground the organization in that case for change.

Chapter Two is on developing strategic alignment. This is the shared intention to accomplish something in the environment that the organization is not currently doing. This compelling vision for the future is the force that will mobilize the organization to change.

Chapter Three presents a leadership network through which local leaders can begin forming individual visions for the future. This is a sustaining and guiding activity that begins to enable the larger organization's change.

Chapter Four describes a role network through which change agents and engagement teams are established throughout the organization. This provides a supplemental information and thought network that allows dialogue around the change, as well as enables the subsequent design efforts.

Chapter Five begins the shift into understanding the systems of the organization. This is a process of engaging a large group of people to begin conceptualizing the systems and processes involved in the change and beginning the creative process necessary for design.

Chapter Six builds off the work of Chapter Five and formalizes the system and process thinking into a provisional design. The chapter is focused on design intents and joint optimization of the business, processes, and people.

Chapter Seven begins the shift from a provisional design to the planning processes required to complete the design. This is a phase shift from design thoughts to design completion, and the engagement expands throughout the organization.

Chapter Eight is focused on establishing the metrics required for the new system.

Chapter Nine is an outline of the work of transition management and the areas of focus needed to maintain a constant design intent and engagement strategy.

Chapter Ten provides an outline of action learning as a change strategy. This is the thread that enables all of the change processes for the organization to take place. The chapter is focused on the action learning cycle and how it operates in an organization.

Chapter Eleven provides a summary checklist of the Ten Tasks, highlighting the areas of work within each task, as well as the critical outputs for each.

Acknowledgments

My thanks to the many people who have significantly impacted my work and, subsequently, this book. I would like to thank my friends, co-workers, and colleagues who supported me through graduate school and my many career shifts. I would also like to mention my colleagues at the Gestalt Institute, who pushed me personally to think about organizations differently. I also want to thank my clients, who have taught me as I have tried to teach them. My thanks to my co-author, who has been a willing teacher, learner, and friend through our many years of work together. Most importantly, I want to thank my wife, Deborah, and children, Vanessa and James, for supporting me though all of my work.

My thanks to you all,

JEFF EVANS

At this point in my work life, I would like to thank the defense department/aerospace industry complex of yesteryear for being confused enough to drive me into graduate studies to try to figure out what ought to be going on. I'd like to express my gratitude to Eric Trist and Bob Tannenbaum for introducing me to a better way, my graduate colleagues for helping me turn abstract concepts into practical adventures, and the ensuing string of clients who have really written this book by demanding that I continue to learn along with them and organize my thinking in our work together.

I'd also like to express special appreciation to my co-author for his hard work and dedication in making sure we got over the hurdles and had this book published.

Thank you,

CHUCK SCHAEFER

Together, we would also like to acknowledge and thank Marsh Clegg—a past client, a recent colleague, and a sounding board for this work. His executive's view of change leadership and his personal insights have helped us in immeasurable ways. We would also like to acknowledge and thank Jennifer Bell, who tirelessly proofed, researched, and assembled our work into a real book, both cheering us on and keeping our noses to the grindstone as we struggled to finish in the midst of life's other commitments. Finally, we would like to acknowledge the team at Jossey-Bass/Pfeiffer, in particular, Matt Holt—for making this book possible—and Susan Rachmeler—for her diligent reviews, her helpful feedback, her firm guidance, and especially her patience with our perpetual pushing of the deadlines in our work on the manuscript.

0

Chapter Zero

To some people "Chapter Zero" may sound a little odd. We have given that title to this opening chapter for two reasons. First, the first step in your organization change work is in Chapter One, the next chapter. Chapter Zero picks you up at "ground zero," what you need to understand about the material in this book before you address that first step. Chapter Zero gives you the overall framework around which this book is formed and the critical beliefs about people and organizations facing change that underpin all of what you will read here. Second, it is titled Chapter Zero simply so that the following chapter titles can match the numbers of the change tasks they address, Chapter One addresses Task I, Chapter Five addresses Task V, and so forth.

About Changing Organizations

Changing is what organizations do, not what you do to them. Changing is the continuous process of an organization attempting to align itself with shifts in its marketplace and with the realities of its external financial, physical, social, political, and technological environment. It is the organization's drive to synchronize purpose, process, structures, people, information, rewards, and management systems within itself and within an integrated outside world.

Organization change can be complex because organizations are complex. Guiding successful intentional change can be puzzling and difficult because the organization is held in place by networks of established interrelationships among its environment, its processes, its structure, and its people. Whether an imperative for change comes from business needs, technological opportunities, mismatches in structural alignment, or the nature of the organization's people, for the change to be lasting, all aspects and interrelationships of the affected networks will have to change. We'll talk more about this "work system" view of organizations in the next chapter and throughout the book.

In yesterday's world, major organization change was often experienced as a cataclysmic eruption one hoped would only happen every millennium or two. In today's more complex, dynamic world, organization change is ongoing work, not just a one-time "catch up" event. Being an agile change artist is as critical for success as being a reliable producer. Successful change is required for survival. Changing more responsively and effectively than one's competitors is required to prosper.

About the People in a Change Situation

Changing organizations are complex because people are complex. People tend to objectify their work. They experience it as separate from themselves, something "out there" that they examine and "work on." They may engage their work with passion, but they still tend to see it as something apart from themselves, something they "do" rather than who they are. A change situation replaces the microscope with a mirror. The prospect of change confronts people with the reality that they are not separate from their work, that in a deeper sense they are what they do and they are defined by how they do it. The task of self-reflection is more complex than the task of objective problem solving. The work of changing organizations is not only about finding a way to apply a logical process to a nonlinear reality, but it is also about setting the conditions within which people are willing to do research on themselves.

The Work of Changing Organizations

Conventional wisdom tells us that changing our organizations is very difficult. That's because we built them in a complex way, not because change is mysterious and unfathomable. Changing an organization is hard work because organizations, and the people who inhabit them, are designed to provide stability. When we put our organizations together, we are looking for predictability. We know we may have to be nimble in a fast-moving marketplace, but at the same time we want to be sure that promises made will be promises met. Our work systems are designed to "ingest" variance without losing control of the process. We pay our people to pursue the objectives tenaciously in spite of the odds. We struggle with change, not because our organizations aren't agile, but because they are so agile in order to stay on course and avoid the rocks in the roadway. Organizations are hard to change because the organization designers before us and the managers who followed them have done their jobs so well.

Changing organization may be hard work, but it doesn't have to be mysterious. In this book, the work involved in changing organization is modeled as "The Ten Tasks of Changing Organization," illustrated by the ten activity bars in Figure 0.1.

The overlapping bars in the model signify that, although the tasks flow sequentially in concept, the work addressing any one task will continue concurrently with the work associated with previous and subsequent tasks as the process unfolds. Picture the overall Ten Tasks as a cascade of activity, like a step-down waterfall, where each level feeds the next and each builds on the flow from before. As a change unfolds, you must cycle over and over through the essence of all of the tasks as you drill down into the details at different levels of the work system or open up change in different parts of the

Figure 0.1. The Ten Tasks of Changing Organization.

I   Appreciating the Situation

II   Developing Strategic Alignment

III   Evoking Change Leadership

IV   Expanding Understanding and Commitment

V   Analyzing Processes

VI   Designing Processes, Work, and Boundaries

VII   Planning Implementation

VIII   Establishing Metrics

IX   Managing Transitions

X   Continuous Learning and Improvement

organization. This is what we mean by saying the process of change may be approached logically, but it is not linear.

The Ten Tasks is not a "methodology" and not a step-by-step process for managing change activities. It is more useful when seen as an overarching checklist of what to pay attention to as you apply your own logical thinking to accomplish the change. An analogy is the early computer game called *Dungeons and Dragons*. I never got the hang of it, but my son was pretty intense about it. As I understand, you are given a general idea about a journey and a bundle of weapons and tools that you can apply as you run into the unexpected beasts of the passageway, the bottomless pit, the unseeable door, the unclimbable wall, and so forth. If what you try doesn't work, you adjust your tactics and try again. As you learn and succeed, you progress and are given more tools and weapons and more insight about how to apply them to the next unexpected challenge, and the challenges just keep coming and coming. Stewardship in changing organization is a little like playing *Dungeons and Dragons*. The Ten Tasks gives you an overview of the path and some good ideas (your weapons and tools) to work with. The bad news is that only you can figure out how to apply them, using your own and your colleagues' best judgments, as the adventure unfolds and the specific challenges come up.

The chapters in this book address each of the ten tasks in order. Chapter Eleven provides a checklist of the work to be undertaken during each task. It can serve as a memory jogger, helping you as you work your way through your change effort. Or you can hand it to another person as a quick outline to guide discussion about where you have been, what has and has not been accomplished so far, and where to go next.

Application of the Ten Tasks Model

How much rigor and attention you must pay to each item listed under each of the ten tasks will depend on its relevance for the situation and the magnitude of the changes you face. For example, in a technology change, the more business process boundaries crossed, the greater the change of skills and knowledge demanded, the larger the impact on collateral systems, and the deeper the impact on culture and careers of the workforce, the more formal attention you must pay to the ten tasks. We'll talk more about the impact of change in Chapter Two.

How collaboratively you approach your change process will also influence how to best work with the Ten Tasks. If you approach the change with high employee involvement, you can often "feed a number of birds with one hand," and many activities can address objectives catalogued under a number of different tasks. For example, in a four-day working conference, a 180-person "deep diagonal slice" (people from multiple levels in the organization's hierarchy and across the span of its horizontal business units) worked together to digest data about present operations, identify trends in the environment, define priorities, agree on the critical elements of a vision for a better future, set "next-step" follow-up actions, and establish plans for their personal involvement in communicating the outcomes of the conference to the rest of the organization. In this single event, they were able to address objectives under Tasks I, II, III, and IV of the Ten Tasks simultaneously.

During the last decade, pioneering efforts in the design of large-group processes for organization development work, such as those of Marv Weisbord and Sandra Janoff, Kathleen Dannemiller and Robert Jacobs, Dick and Emily Axelrod, Bill Pasmore, Harrison Owen, and the earlier work of Fred Emery and Erick Trist, have made high involvement and collaboration in organization analysis, design, and development much more practical. Our successful experience in building on the work of these pioneers has allowed us to, figuratively speaking, "get the whole system in the room at the same time," as in the example above, and to accelerate the time it takes to accomplish, diffuse, and establish critical decisions about the state of things and the directions to pursue in a change effort. Two good overviews of these pioneering large-group processes are the books *Large Group Interventions* (Bunker & Alban, 1997) and *The Change Handbook* (Holman & Devane, 1999).

Core Beliefs That Shape Our Practice

There are a few simple beliefs about change that have guided us in our most successful change work. Whenever we violate the principles represented in them, because of time pressure or opposition, the effectiveness of the process has suffered. As my grandmother used to say, "Pay me now or pay me later!"

People Change Because They Choose to Change

For organizations and the people who inhabit them, changing is choice, changing is work, and changing is learning. Guiding change in organizations, therefore, is not just the business of designing new technologies, structures, and behaviors and training people to use them. Guiding change has more to do with establishing the context within which people can really engage the needed changes, and the primary rule of thumb for that engagement was succinctly stated a long time ago by our colleague Frank Delaney in his paraphrase of an old axiom about communication:

> "*Tell me*—I may hear; I may remember.
> *Show me*—I may understand better.
> *Involve me*—I will take ownership; I will add value and be committed."

The Overarching Goal of Any Change in an Organization Is Constant

No matter what your specific change objectives are, the overarching goal is *always* to move toward a higher and higher performing work system. Or else why bother? In any change effort, it is easy to become locked into immediate objectives and to become focused on the immediate struggles to accomplish them. However, it is worth coming up for air every once in a while and reaffirming what you are ultimately trying to do.

An Organization Is a Work System

Re-emphasizing what we said earlier, an organization is a work system. Its relationship with its environment and the behavior of its people and processes are held in place by a network of structures, interrelationships, demands, and consequences that make up that system. The major imperative for change may come from business needs, technological opportunities, mismatches in structural alignment, or the nature of the organization's people. However, for the intended change to take hold, all the related aspects of the network will have to be addressed.

Implementation of Change Begins with the First Encounter

Implementation starts when you first encounter a stakeholder about the possibility of change. Implementation is not just a project step that follows design, not a problem you address when you are ready to "roll out" your changes. It is much more than "selling" changes to the stakeholders and looking for buy-in. It is an integral part of how you approach everything you do in each task. You have to keep this clearly in mind as you plan your work and work your plan. The world is a stage, and the audience begins reacting to the play with the first crack of the curtain. There are no dress rehearsals in real life.

Successful Change Is an Informed, Open Process

Communicate! Communicate! Communicate! In a change situation, secrecy is an illusion. If people don't know the specific details, they will invent them, and we human beings tend to splash our blank canvasses with our worst nightmares. If people don't know what's going on, they cannot help make it come out right. So when you are sick and tired of saying something, say it again. When you are sure you have all the information you need, ask the question at least once more. When you are sure you have reached a mutual understanding, discuss it again. When you think you have planned enough interactions into a process, double the plan. Most importantly, remember that simple distribution of information is the business of a newspaper and that change leadership is not just journalism. Communication is a two-way street, not just telling and selling, not just a series of well-engineered messages that you want people to believe in. It includes listening and a dialogue about meaning.

Change Leadership Is Guiding Collaborative Action Learning

Although we may not believe we are very good at leading organization change, we know how to lead people in becoming clear about objectives, planning and taking action, collecting data about what happened, making sense of the results, learning from our successes and failures, and re-planning as conditions dictate. This is the rhythm of *action learning,* and action learning is the fundamental rhythm of successful change (Lewin, 1947). As change leaders, we must start with the mind-set of guiding a collaborative action learning process, rather than trying to plan activities that will change people's behavior. The rhythm of action learning is discussed more deeply in Chapter Ten. If the thought of leading change from a learning perspective intrigues you, but you don't have much experience with this approach, you may want to read Chapter Ten next instead of Chapter One, because the notion of *organization change as organizational learning* underpins this book.

For Change to Last, It Has to Optimize Business, Process, and Human Requirements Jointly

There was a time when you could "make it" in Hollywood if you were very good looking, could really act, or could sing and dance like gangbusters. Today, it seems you need to have all three attributes just to get into the casting interviews. That's a metaphor for business in today's environment. You used to be able to focus your attention on strict supervision of processes and *inspect* your way to consistency of product at the expense of human and material costs. Or you used to be able to push your processes to maximum volume at the cost of quality and human frustration. Or you used to be able to provide exceptional quality through increasing individual rewards, inflating prices, and diminishing quantity. *Not any more!* Today, every system improvement and work design decision has to embody a joint optimization of reliably delivering products at competitive costs, controlling the processes to control consistency, *and* providing the quality of work life required to attract the energy and commitment of the work force required to do it.

Summary

The work of change begins with an individual believing that something should be different. Moving from the individual to an organization requires stewardship of the change process. The work of changing organizations can be complex because organizations are complex. However, the work of changing organization can be modeled as ten major tasks and approached systematically. What you believe about change and about people set the conditions for how you conduct yourself in the change steward's role. Your behavior heavily influences the conditions of the change situation. So one of the opportunities you have in reading this book and applying its content is to examine your own beliefs about yourself, about people, and about changing organization. Here are a few key beliefs that have served the authors well in our change work:

- People change because they choose to change

- The overarching goal of any organization change is constant—high performance

- An organization is a *work system*; for change to take hold it has to address all the elements

- Implementation of change begins with the first encounter

- Successful change is an informed, open process

- Change leadership is guiding collaborative action learning

- For change to last, it has to optimize business, process, and human requirements jointly

1

Task I: Appreciating the Situation

Getting Started

Probably a hundred management writings and perhaps a thousand self-help guides start with, "There is an old Chinese proverb that a journey of a thousand miles begins with the first step." It may be worn threadbare, but it's still a meaningful insight. One of the important messages imbedded in that old saw is, "Even if the prospect seems huge, and you don't know everything about it, quit diddling around and just get started!" As an old friend from Louisiana used to say, "If you want to run with the big dogs, you've got to get off of the porch." Another message is in the proverb, "Take the meal a mouthful at a time." Alan Lakein (1973), an early leader in the field of personal achievement and time management, called it "*Swiss-cheesing* the overwhelming 'A' priority task." It means poking a few holes in the task by getting on with what you can do *now*. That's one of the things this book is all about, breaking the big projects into manageable ones without losing touch with the whole picture. A third message is that you can't really know the path until you engage it or, as Kurt Lewin is credited with saying, "If you really want to understand an organization, try to change it." That's another proposition in this book, approaching organization change as a learning journey. We would add a corollary, "You can't really know what you want until you engage the challenges of going after what you think it is."

So what's in Task I, this first step on your change journey? It's developing a feeling for the general state of your organization, the situation it faces, the imperatives for change, and the magnitude of the change needed. At this early stage, you are looking for broad-level but meaningful understanding. This is not the time to dive down into the details. Depth and precision will evolve later. What you want now is a good initial estimate of the potential scope and difficulties of the changes in store for you. This understanding will form the basis for your approach, decisions, and visioning in Task II.

In this chapter, we highlight six major pieces of Task I work that you must plan and accomplish in order to develop your appreciation of the situation (and don't forget the "Swiss cheese"). These six pieces are

- Understanding your organization's environment, the alignment of your purpose or "mission" in relation to it, and your present and historical performance

- Examining the state of your organization's major processes and practices and prioritizing problems and gaps

- Estimating the scope and impact of the changes needed to fix misalignments, address problems, and close the gaps

- Estimating the magnitude of the change stewardship work to move ahead

- Judging the organization's readiness and past experience with these kinds of change

- Defining the potential benefits and costs of changing and preparing a compelling business-based case for change

Approaching the Organization As a Work System

Serious expansion of open systems thinking in organization was stimulated by the publication of Katz and Kahn's book, *The Social Psychology of Organizations,* originally published in 1966 and still available in paperback (Katz & Kahn, 1978) or in an updated hardcover edition (Katz & Kahn, 1990). As referenced in a valuable little paper by Russell Ackoff (1994), "Systems Thinking and Thinking Systems," the thinking goes back at least to the 1940s with the work of Ludwig von Bertalanffy (1968).

As for our job here, it will help structure the effort of Task I if you have a simple systems model of organization to work from. McKinsey & Company's "7-S Model" (Peters & Waterman, 1982), Hanna's "Organization Performance Model" (1988), Nadler's "Congruence Model" (Nadler, Gerstein, & Shaw, 1992), and Galbraith's "Star Model" (1994) are all examples.

"The Organization Wheel" illustrated in Figure 1.1 is a work system model that we have developed over time and find particularly easy to apply in an organization development effort. The shape of the model began to evolve in our early work with systems thinking in organization. It took form through a fascination with the Native American Plains Indian People's "Medicine Wheel Circle," which represents the universe of change and harmony with everything around us (Storm, 1972). We use The Organization Wheel, referred to as "The Wheel," in several ways throughout our discussion of the Ten Tasks. The first application is in this chapter to help structure the work of Task I.

• *Alignment with the Environment.* This element focuses on the wants, values, and quality criteria of the organization's major stakeholders; the organization's competitive position and the quality of its relationships and transactions with the major stakeholders; and the dynamics and future trends in the environment and the implications of those trends for the organization (its strategic drivers).

Figure 1.1. The Organization Wheel.

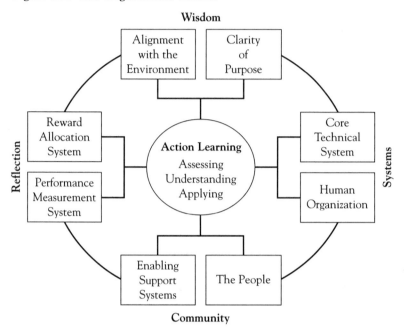

• *Clarity of Purpose.* This element includes the organization's defining values, core mission, and vision for the future; its strategic intent in relation to the strategic drivers in its environment and the critical success factors for achieving that intent; its strategies and plans for achieving its goals; and the qualities of its core products in relation to those strategies and plans.

• *Core Technical System.* This element covers the input and output requirements of the transformation processes that produce the organization's core products; its technologies and practices for controlling the variance in those processes; the information, knowledge, skills, capabilities, and issue resolution practices required to operate, maintain, and manage contingencies and upgrade those processes to match the demands and dynamics of the environment.

- *Human Organization.* This element contains the organization's role structure, processes, boundary locations, and network of relationships for accomplishing and supporting the core transformation process, dealing with the environment, supporting the people, and adapting to the future.

- *The People.* This element includes the beliefs, attitudes, and values of those who populate the human system; their knowledge, skills, and capabilities; their culture, personalities, and diversity; their career expectations; their quality of work life (QWL) expectations; and their support needs.

- *Enabling Support Systems.* This element contains the organization's technical and human process support systems, information systems, maintenance and supply systems, systems for developing personal and organizational effectiveness, and access, control, and authority allocation processes.

- *Performance Measurement System.* This element focuses on measurement and assessment of outcomes and behaviors (business, technical, and human) in relation to the organization's defining values, core mission, vision for the future, strategic intent, and the strategies and plans for achieving its goals.

- *Reward Allocation System.* This element addresses the distribution of the benefits of participation among the stakeholders in the enterprise (external and internal), the processes for allocating and distributing those benefits, and the relationship between rewards and performance.

- *Action Learning.* In this element are the processes of applied learning for accomplishment, alignment, integration, continuous improvement, adapting, mastery, and renewal.

As a side note, The Wheel models the processes of your organization; those of your technical system (the value-adding transformation of input into final product); and those of your human system (called "Human Organization" in the model) as separate yet highly interdependent networks. This comes from sociotechnical systems thinking in the development of high-performance organizations. The knowledge generated in that field has strongly influenced our work from the beginning. If you are interested in deepening your understanding of that approach, two books, *Performance by Design* by Jim Taylor and David Felten (1993) and *Designing a High-Performance Organization* by Bill Lytle (1998), have good mixes of theory and discussion of methodology. For a definitive overview, go to *The Social Engagement of Social Science Volume II: The Socio-Technical Perspective* (Trist, Emery, & Murray, 1993).

Approaching Task I As a Dialogue

It would be wise to approach Task I as a dialogue rather than as just a data-gathering exercise. Appreciating an organizational situation involves scanning at all levels of the system. However, perspectives focused on individuals trying to meet personal responsibilities, focused on an organization trying to accommodate as a whole, or focused on a business in a dynamic and unintegrated environment will be different. People looking from those different viewpoints will see different things. In addition, filling a role in an organizational structure guarantees tunnel vision. People who embark on Task I will be working from their own unique experience of what is important to themselves and what they believe should be important to others. An executive may place more emphasis on the overall output and financials. People in a dicey situation may unconsciously emphasize security or quality of work life. Engineering groups may be more drawn to the technical possibilities than to the pragmatic realities. Marketers may experience the world more as a customer, rather than as an internal supplier. When you stir up all their information in the mixer of dialogue, you not only get richer realities, but you get the different parts beginning to listen to the whole. Implementation of change has begun and, if done with sensitivity, the parts begin to open up to new realities. People start to explore new ideas and to practice suspending personal judgment (Senge, 1990).

We have a little dilemma here, a good example of how the Ten Tasks cannot be used as a simple step-by-step methodology. If you go back and review the pieces of work proposed for Task I, you will see that they flow in a logical sequence, each building on the former to develop the knowledge and momentum for change. But here you are, at the very first step on the journey, asking people to commit their time and energy to a dialogue about change that you don't build a case for until the end of this task. You are asking managers to commit resources to a change task, and you don't get around to "evoking" their change leadership until Task III. You are asking people to participate in thoughtful self-reflection, and you won't know how they feel about doing that until much later. You are asking people to assess the state of their processes before they learn where and how to look at them in Task V. You are asking them to ignore their pain and think about the possibilities before they have developed a vision of a better place. And finally, you will have to define the potential benefits and costs of changing before you get around to developing your vision of where you are going in Task II and the real bottom-line information about that in Tasks V, VI, and VII.

You will have to work through these issues and do the best you can. Remember the old Chinese proverb and the part about not being able to know the path and what you should do until you engage it and discover the challenge.

Assessing the Alignment of Your Environment and Your Purpose

This is where to go first, with the "wisdom" of your enterprise, represented by the interrelationship of the two elements at the north (top) of The Wheel—your environment and your purpose. It is tempting to begin with your "pain," exploring the problems you face, but it works out better to begin with your reason for being. After all, how will you know what your problems really are if you don't know what you are up to? Besides, in an organization change effort, you do not want to get cornered into just solving problems. You are trying to build a work system that can achieve its goals and regularly solve its problems as part of the job. There is one caveat here, however: People *want* to talk about their problems with willing listeners. If there is garbage in the system, it will be hard for them to put a lot of energy into what can seem to be pretty abstract or high-level concepts such as "environment and purpose." You may have to find a way to validate their feelings without distracting from your objectives, before you can get their serious input and dialogue.

Now, back to getting a good handle on the state of your organization's *wisdom*. One of the fundamentals of organization work is the fit between the organization and the environment. All organizations are in continual interplay with the external world. The organization acts on the environment, learns from it, and adapts. The environment acts on the organization, learns from it, and is changed. How you and your organization apply what you learn and adapt can be more strategic and more under your control than can how a nonintegrated environment beyond your control will adjust to you. So we suggest that you first look outside at what you have to match, then inside at your purpose and what you want to do. Without some sense of purpose, however, an environmental scan can be all over the map, overwhelming in size, and hold little real interest for the explorers. You must have some way to focus and scan without overly limiting the possibilities for discovery.

Here are a few questions to consider in making your initial assessment about the environment and your purpose in it. As you answer these questions, make note of the mismatches or gaps you may ultimately have to address and keep track of any ideas about fixes that pop out (although you want to discourage specific effort in this area).

About the Stakeholders in Your Environment

- Who are the principal direct investors, customers, suppliers, and outside regulators of your organization's core processes?

- What do they expect from you and what do they value that leads them to have these expectations? (The latter half of this question leads to insights into why they want what they say they need and opens possibilities for meeting their more fundamental requirements in better ways.)

- What do you want from them and what do you value that leads you to want these things?

- What is the quality of your transactions and working relations with these principal stakeholders?

- What is your present and historical performance in meeting their expectations?

About Your Organization's Sense of Purpose

- What are the mission and vision of excellence for this organization?

- What core values (business, process, and quality of work life) are represented in your vision?

- What are the critical success factors for accomplishing your mission and realizing your vision?

- How well are these things understood across your organization, and how influential are they in guiding the day-to-day actions of your people?

About the Dynamics and Trends in Your Environment

- What dynamics and trends in the environment may be

important to understand and track, given your sense of purpose?

- Which of these do you believe to be the really significant "strategic drivers" in your environment?

- Does this change what you just identified as your critical success factors? In what way?

About Your Strategies and Plans

- What are your strategies and business plans for living up to the critical success factors you have identified?

- How well are these understood across your organization, and how influential are they in guiding the day-to-day actions of your people?

- What is your present and historical performance in meeting your objectives?

About Misalignments and Gaps

- What misalignments, gaps, or unknowns exist regarding your intentions and the demands of your environment?

- What are the highest priorities to address, given your understanding of the strategic drivers in your environment and your critical success factors?

- Are you facing systems improvement or fundamental renewal?

Examining Your Processes and Practices

For this work, you move your focus clockwise around The Wheel, first to explore your Technical and Human Systems in the east (right) and then on to the People and Support Systems in the south (bottom). At this early stage, you probably won't need to look deeply into the other three elements—measurement, reward, and learning—in the west (left), unless the major driver for change is coming from one of these elements.

Here are a few questions that might help you develop a good, high-level assessment of the state of your processes. Again, as you answer these questions make note of the mismatches or gaps you may ultimately have to address and keep track of any ideas about fixes that pop out (although you want to discourage specific effort in this area).

About Your Core Products

- Referring to the work you did addressing Alignment with the Environment and Clarity of Purpose, what are your major stakeholders' critical specifications for the core products and services you provide?

About the Core Processes That Provide Your Core Products

- How reliably do your core processes deliver on the critical specifications?

About the Structure and Processes of Your Human Organization

- How well do the distribution of roles and the boundaries of your organization support high performance in planning for the future, controlling your core processes, and dealing with your environment?

- How is the work that has to be accomplished by this organization identified, prioritized, scheduled, and allocated? How effective are the processes?

- How are information and authority dispersed to accomplish the work effectively? How well is this working?

- How are coordination and alignment across the internal boundaries of your organization accomplished? How well is it working?

About the People

- How well do the skills, capacities, and culture of your workforce match up to the needs of the organization, as implied by your answers to the questions so far?

- What new key attributes in the work force are required?

- How similar to and different from present attributes are they?

- What are the "reinforcements" in your organizational environment that either support or deter the behaviors that would reflect the required key attributes?

About Your Organization's Support Systems

- How well do your organization's support systems facilitate:

  Maintaining your clarity of purpose and alignment with the environment?

  The information flow, communications, and coordination necessary to plan and control your core processes and deal effectively with your environment?

  Supporting the personal needs of the people?

- Are your support systems built to support your core processes or do they seem to have a life of their own?

Summarizing Misalignments, Gaps, and Problems

Some of the questions above could require detailed analysis to answer adequately. At this early stage in the Ten Tasks, intuitive answers by people intimately involved in the issues in day-to-day work life can often serve you just fine. Regardless of how the data is generated, you have to make a meaningful overall summary using a range of viewpoints. We have found that large-group approaches can work very well in making this summary. What you are searching for are answers to the following questions:

- What misalignments, gaps, and problems do you see between your fundamental sense of purpose and the nature of your environment?

- What misalignments, gaps, and problems do you see between the outcomes of your processes and the critical requirements of your stakeholders?

- What misalignments, gaps, and problems do you see among the needs of your processes, the structure of your organization, and the attributes of your people?

- What are the highest priorities to address, given the strategic drivers in your environment and your critical success factors?

- Are you facing systems improvement or fundamental renewal?

Estimating the Scope and Impact of Potential Changes

At this stage of the process, estimating the scope of the potential change is probably an intuitive piece of work. You want to invite creative thinking but not to generate reams of junk. The players won't have much tolerance for that. Also, you don't want to zero in on a specific "fix" just yet, but there still has to be sufficient reality and credibility in this judgment to complete the work of Task I.

Again, large-group processes employing subject-matter experts from multiple levels of the organization may help you finish this piece of work expeditiously and with credibility. Regardless of how you approach it, we suggest you use The Wheel to structure your exploration and keep track of the potential changes on each of the elements. We recommend that you again start in the north (top) and progress clockwise. Start with the summary of misalignments, gaps, and problems from the prior piece of work and make your best judgments about the best ways to address these. This might be a very good time to feed in thought-provoking ideas from outside your organization and explore things others have done or thought about. What's worked well and what hasn't lived up to its promises? What future kinds of things are being thought about out there? We remember one client talking about needing "out of the box" thinking, and his colleague saying, "We've been out of the box for a long time because the box has moved and we're just sitting here!"

To get a good feeling for the impact of potential changes as you work your way around the circle, add in the implications for change in any of the other elements suggested by the change in the element you are focused on. For example, say you have identified a potential need for new technology in your core system or a major support system. What are the implications for the people? What about authority structure or reward systems? How might it drain from the requirements to maintain present technologies or place pressure on resources and capital allocated to other initiatives? How does it fit into the present business plans? How does it match up with trends in the environment?

There is a big change stewardship caution here. Keep this work substantive and meaningful, but keep it light. The reason that most of these things haven't been addressed before is not because they are slipping by without being noticed. It's more likely they are in the "overwhelming A" category because of magnitude or cost or special interests, and people have been doing whatever it takes to work around them. A pile of overwhelming A's on the chest can stop a body from breathing. So do whatever it takes to keep your Swiss cheese palatable and stay in touch with your senior sponsorship for their support during this task.

One other useful caution: Avoid getting trapped in extensive overanalysis here. It's a common way that organizations try to "out wait" the forces for change and miss the boat.

Estimating the Magnitude of the Change Effort

When you go forward in Task II with the business case for change developed at the end of Task I, the people are not only going to ask what's changing, but how they are going to go about it and what it will cost. Part of the estimate will be based on the resources it will take to design and install the physical aspects of the changes. A second part of the estimate will be based on the resources it will take to manage the human resources administration work required for restructuring, moving, downsizing or upsizing, and adjusting skills in the workforce. The final part of the estimate will depend on how you approach all of the other aspects and what special things you may have to do because of the change stewardship implications of the situation.

You will have a better idea about your resource requirements after you identify your high-level approach defined in Task II and create a more detailed plan in Task IV. At this phase of a change effort, all of your resource estimates can be pretty rough, but they will have to be made. Our best advice is to take your best guess at the costs definable for parts one and two above, then add between 10 and 50 percent, based on where you judge that the changes fall on the four "rules of thumb" change impact slopes shown in Figures 1.2 through 1.5. It gets a little hard for pragmatic managers to swallow that kind of a figure, but again, as my dear old grandmother used to say, "Pay me now or pay me later." What an organization tries to save in up-front time and money by efficiency in the approach often is eaten up in the full life-cycle costs from resistance to the change and under-utilization of its potential benefits.

The figures illustrating the organizational impact slopes for changes in each of four major aspects of organization versus the importance of change stewardship and systematic application of the Ten Tasks are shown below. These are purely our intuitive qualitative judgments about what happens in a change effort based on our experience.

Business and Environment Changes. The more you move from straightforward product changes through changes in the way you handle transactions with your environment to repositioning yourself in a new industry, the more the impact on the organization and the more attention you will pay to change stewardship issues. The greater the number of stakeholders impacted, the greater the number and diversity of other businesses and competitors impacted; and the greater the depth of the stakeholder cultural impact, the more rigor and structure required to address change stewardship issues (see Figure 1.2).

Technical System Changes. In change to *technical systems*, the more you move from straightforward process improvement through major process redesign to fundamental systems reengineering, the more rigor and formality you will have to use in planning for the change stewardship implications. The greater the number of organizational boundaries crossed by *technical system* change, the greater the impact on collateral and interfacing technical systems; and the greater the depth of cultural change implied for the stakeholders by

Figure 1.2. Business Issues.

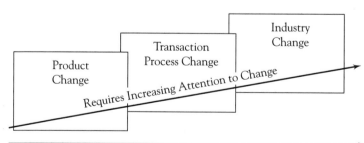

- Increasing Number of Stakeholders
- Increasing Number and Diversity of Businesses
- Increasing Depth of Stakeholder Cultural Impact

your *technical system* change, the more stakeholder involvement and change leadership required (see Figure 1.3).

Human Organization Changes. In change to the structures and processes of the *human organization*, the more you move from the work group level through the business unit level to the whole organization with the changes, the more attention and sophistication you will need to put into change stewardship. The greater the number and diversity of functions involved, the greater the number and diversity of people involved, and the greater the depth of cultural change required of the people, the more planning, structure, and change leadership you will need (see Figure 1.4).

Figure 1.3. Technical Issues.

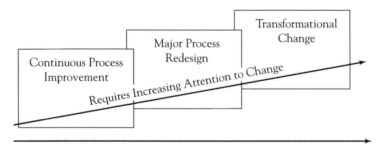

- Increasing Number of Boundaries Crossed
- Increasing Impact on Collateral Systems
- Increasing Depth of Cultural Change

Figure 1.4. Human System Issues.

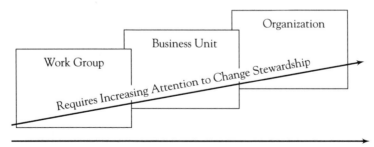

- Increasing Number and Diversity of Functions Involved
- Increasing Number and Diversity of People Affected
- Increasing Depth of Cultural Change

People Changes. With *the people*, the more you move from change in tools and procedures for doing the work through shifts in roles and responsibilities to changes in work affiliations and career paths, the more planning, stakeholder engagement, and leadership you will require for successful change. The greater the number and diversity of people and disciplines affected, the greater the level of skills and knowledge demanded, and the greater the impact on cultural beliefs, personal values, and career expectations, the more attention you will need to pay to change stewardship (see Figure 1.5). To get an idea of the scope and type of change involved, all of these must be taken together. You can use a form like the one in Exhibit 1.1 to capture your thoughts and document your findings.

Judging the Organization's Readiness for Change

There are scores of different beliefs, definitions, models, propositions, and sensing instruments related to people's state of readiness and capacity for change. The knowledge and information are important for the stewards of change because, like the four factors above, it will significantly influence how they work with a change situation. We know of no better model for organizing your thinking around this issue than Dick Beckhard's "change equation," which he credits to David Gleicer (Beckhard, 1978). Simply stated,

Figure 1.5. People Issues.

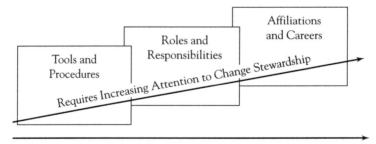

- Increasing Number and Diversity of People and Disciplines Impacted
- Increasing Level of Skills and Knowledge Required
- Increasing Depth of Cultural Change

Exhibit 1.1. Planning for Complex Change.

Proposed Change:

Stakeholder:

Area of Impact	Statement of Impact	Low	Medium	High
Business Issues		Product	Transaction Process	Industry
What is changing?				
How many stakeholders are impacted?				
How many different businesses are impacted?				
What is the depth of stakeholder cultural impact?				
Technical System Issues		Continuous Improvement	Major Process Redesign	Transformational Change
What is the desired impact?				
How many existing boundaries are crossed?				

Exhibit 1.1. Planning for Complex Change, Cont'd.

Area of Impact	Statement of Impact	Low	Medium	High
How are collateral systems impacted?				
What is the depth of cultural impact?				
Human System Issues		Work Group	Business Unit	Organization
What is the desired impact?				
How many existing functions are involved?				
How many people are affected?				
What is the depth of cultural impact?				
People Issues		Tools & Procedures	Roles & Responsibility	Affiliations & Careers
What is the desired impact?				
How many existing boundaries are crossed?				
What level of skills is required?				
What is the depth of cultural impact?				

the equation proposes that the amount of change and the people's appetite for it (Δ) will be a function of how much (= ƒ) the level of dissatisfaction with the status quo (D), times the clarity of the vision about a better state (V), times the clarity of a plan for practical first steps (P) exceeds (>) the perceived cost (C) of the change.

$$\Delta = f \ (D \times V \times P) > C$$

The concept and model have been around for a long time. They are widely recognized and used in the field of organization change and are certainly not unique to our work. The model is easy to grasp and probably gives a change steward or the targets of change most of what they need to assess what they have and do not have in the change situation they face.

Although stated as an equation, the model is not intended to be quantifiable. It is an intuitive proposition to guide qualitative assessment of the change situation through the eyes and feelings of the people in the organization. We prefer trying to understand the status through conversation and dialogue over gathering data by paper-and-pencil opinion surveys. Large-group processes can be useful here. If you really believe that change in organizations is a learning journey, it is as important for the people to learn firsthand about themselves and their system as it is for stewards of change to have the information to use strategically.

The simplest meaning of the model is that if D, V, or P is essentially zero, you aren't going very far very fast. Or if the perceived expense of the adventure is experienced as very high, in either personal or resource costs, you aren't going to see much movement either. On your best judgments about the relative magnitude of the components, you can plan interventions that will be most helpful in supporting a valuable change initiative and then determine which interventions might be a waste of time and resources. For example, say people's dissatisfaction with the status quo is relatively high, but that their vision of a better world is limited. In this case, it would probably be more productive to put your resources into validating their concerns and exploring what others have done, rather than into emphasizing the problems they face and asking executives to give speeches about the urgency of the situation. To get a feel for the power in this simple model, take a few minutes to reflect on specific times during change efforts you have been part of when things were going really well. Now think of some times when the change goals were right but the effort was just not progressing. What was happening in each case relative to the change equation? What was done right? What should have been done differently? What might have been approached in another way if the people working for the change had had the model to work from?

Another nice thing about the model is that it invites people to look at what they experience as "resistance" in a different way. Typically, resistance is seen as something to overcome, something subversive to fight against. The change equation invites you to look at what's missing, what the people need to learn to get to the same place the stewards have gone. It can help the change leaders get on the side of the people against the problem, rather than against the people and treating them as if they were the problem (Maurer, 1996; Nevis, 1987).

The cost side of the equation is worth thinking about also, as there are a number of dimensions to "cost." There is the logical part, based on "balancing the checkbook" related to resource requirements, risk assessment, and prioritizing the list of things you want. Then there is the emotional part, based on hopes and personal agendas, experience with similar changes in the past, and trust in the future. Human beings have a marvelous ability to look at a situation and immediately size up intuitively what it might cost. You can work on the logical part by providing more data, by "correcting" their assumptions, by releasing more resources, or by constructing "safety nets," and so forth. However, you can't usually "argue" them out of their emotional positions. Pressure against resistance is met with more resistance. Employees are going to have to believe and trust in the forces for change, and the "forces" have to be people—not faceless groups, not slogans, not sales pitches—they can trust. I remember a man from a major oil company who had been part of a tremendous reengineering of their overall process for oil exploration. What he said has stuck with me and comes to mind often in my work. He said, "The top brass finally stood up in front of us and admitted that they were just learners in this process too. Before, they never would have admitted that and probably were afraid that we would panic if we knew they were struggling too. But you know, I developed more trust in them at that point than ever before, and folks quit bickering with each other and got together on their side against the overwhelming challenges. And now here we are, right where we all wanted to be, right out there ahead of the pack." We talk more about evoking change leadership in Chapter Three.

One last thought about the power of past experience and the perception of possible cost. All people have gone through change in the course of their personal and professional lives. Not all of it has been a pleasant experience. Poorly handled or imposed change tends to leave people bitter about ideas and approaches that were used. Part of a change effort is often allowing people to "work through" their past experience with change, rather than trying to talk them out of it.

To get an idea of how this works, take your proposed change out to a few of your stakeholders and have a dialogue around these areas. Use the form in Exhibit 1.2 to co-create a meaningful engagement plan.

Preparing a Compelling Business-Based Case for Change

Neither organizations nor individuals change without first coming to a realization that something has to be different than it is now. The intensity of the wake-up call is often directly proportional to

Exhibit 1.2. Change Engagement Plan.

Proposed Change:		Primary Responsibility:	
		Support:	

For each stakeholder (or group), find out where he or she is in each of the areas. Work collaboratively to determine an engagement plan for approaching the proposed change.

Stakeholder	D		V		P		C		Engagement Plan

the effort the individual or organization has put into *not* trying to change. In the process of driving for stability, both individuals and organizations can lose touch with what is going on around them. These once-honored champions of stability can quickly become whispered about as the suppressive underminers and resistors of the "glorious vision." They often feel that they are being asked to give up a lot of what they fought so nobly to protect and that there is now disdain rather than admiration for who they are and what they do. Some of these will be very influential and powerful people in the organization. This leads us to the purpose of a compelling business case for change. It is not there to "sell" the process, but to help the champions of stability come to terms with what has been happening around them and throw their weight in the new direction, rather than hanging it out like an anchor. Your business case will be used over and over to explain the changes. One change effort we participated in had several dimensions to its business case:

- *Competitor Benchmarking.* About six months prior to initiating an organization redesign, the company launched a benchmarking effort. Large gaps were indicated in overhead and operating costs. The results and analysis were available by the time the organization redesign was announced.

- *G&A Study.* Results of an earlier G&A study indicated large barriers between departments, leading to redundancy, rework, and frustration among employees.

- *Vision and Mission.* A new customer-focused vision and updated mission for the company required new and more front-line employee-empowered approaches to their operations, which in turn required more employee-involved ways to achieve the changes than the more hierarchical methods traditionally employed.

- *Employee Survey.* A standard employee survey indicated poor employee commitment to the company's efforts.

The combination of new data and a compelling vision provided a solid business case that gave many good reason to support the effort.

Summary

Gaining a greater appreciation of the organization's situation does a great deal to promote change readiness as people become aware of the issues around their current state. That readiness often leads people to want to correct everything they have found immediately. There are two basic issues with moving to problem solving at this point. First, all solutions will be determined based on the known conditions of the current state. The effort will thus move toward re-creating the ideal version of the existing organization, rather than toward exploring new possibilities. Second, this process diffuses the creative energy available to create a shared vision for growth and development. Applying that creative energy toward a different set of conditions than those that currently exist enables transformational change.

The second requirement of change is to create a new image of the organization that all members can move toward. This is the work of Task II.

Points to Remember

Look at the Whole System. Even if the change seems to focus on only one area of the organization, remember that you are dealing with an integrated system, each area of which is operating in some sort of balance with the other areas.

Strive to Highlight What Is. At this point in the change effort, work to point out the conditions that exist in the organization in a non-judgmental and clear fashion. This should be a data flood that speaks for itself. The case for change should be compelling because it is compelling, not because we say it should be.

Use the Change Equation to Plan Your Discussions. The change equation will provide valuable guidance to your conversations and the structure of the case for change.

———————

Common Trip Points

Over-Deploying the Organization's Strengths. Organizations can become stuck simply by over-deploying their particular strengths. In a strongly analytical organization, the practices of the organization may be designed to provide depths of rigor beyond what is necessary to actually run the business. If this is the case in the organization, that same rigor will spill over into the business case for change. Analysis paralysis and action addiction will show up in the practices and will also show up in the work of Task I.

Selling vs. Telling. In preparing the business case for change, the people working are likely to develop strong opinions about where the business should go. It is easy to fall into "selling" that solution through the business case. The business case should tell the story, not sell the solution.

Reacting vs. Proactive Behavior. The most powerful and sustainable change comes from proactively pursuing goals in the environment. Fill the business case with language that is proactive and geared toward a positive goal. Avoid reactionary language and defensive posturing to rationalize existing systems.

Overestimating Trust in Leadership. If the system has low trust in leadership, the people will probably have low trust in the business case for change that this leadership has presented. If you know there is a trust issue with particular leaders, be wary of their early involvement in the business case for change.

2

Task II: Developing
Strategic Alignment

The Work of Task II

The overall work of Task II is establishing a change strategy for your organization. The overall objective of Task II is to exercise your strategy to develop alignment within your organization and with critical elements of the environment about the strategic underpinnings of the change and in how you approach the change process. The specific work of Task II is to apply your communication strategy to doing the following:

- Developing a communication strategy and establish a robust communication network

- Developing a dialogue about the state of the business and the major processes

- Developing a dialogue about the case for change

- Learning about alternatives

- Developing a compelling vision for the future

- Developing a strategy and proposed approach to changing

- Developing a high-level action plan

- Implementing an infrastructure to manage the process

It is not a coincidence that the pieces of work listed above track with the D, V, P, and C categories of the change equation from Chapter One. How you go about the work of Task II, how much effort and formality you put into each piece of work, and where you focus your attention will depend on your appreciation of the situation as you apply the logic of that equation.

Establishing a Communication Network and Strategy

The Role Network

The fundamental role network structure of any planned change effort is shown in Figure 2.1. One of the authors first saw the basics of this model begin to take form on a chalkboard during graduate school. A small group of friends and classmates was trying to help

Figure 2.1. Role Network for Change.

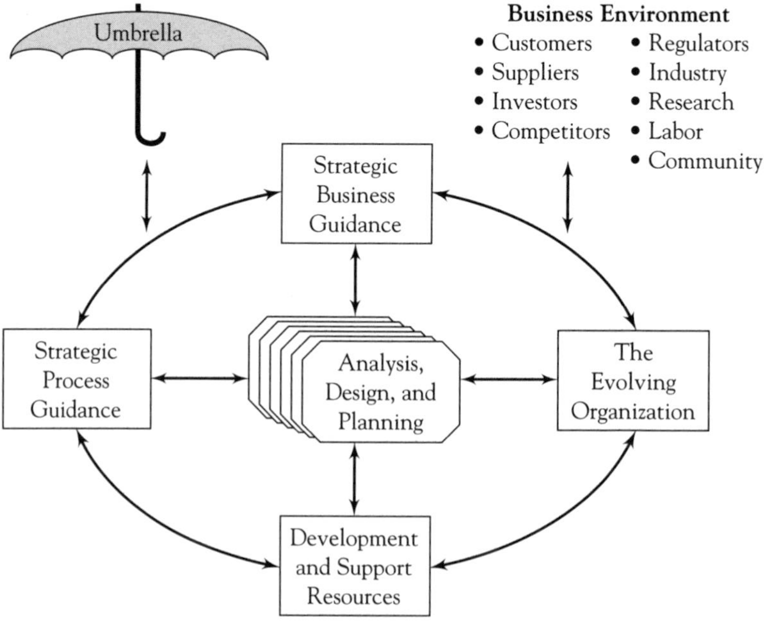

a fellow student structure a data-gathering plan for her dissertation. One member of the group, G.K. Jayaram, went to the board and put the somewhat random advice being tossed at the helpee into the basic form shown in the figure. Jy had a nice way of taking roaming thoughts and forming them into coherent models. This one stuck with us.

The boxes in the role network shown in Figure 2.1 represent the general "who" that needs to be talking to "whom" in a change program. The arrows represent "about what," and your strategy guides how and when. The box at the top of the network provides the program with the basic reason and direction for the change. The box on the left-hand side provides fundamental guidance for the change process, which is what this book is all about. The boxes in the middle accomplish the detailed work of the Ten Tasks, and the box at the right ultimately takes over, finalizes, absorbs, and brings to life the final outcomes. The box at the bottom of the figure stands ready and provides technical and human process development support that is beyond the immediate capability or capacity of the players in the other boxes. The domains in the "business environment" represent locations of critical external stakeholders and major regulators for the work system undergoing change. The "umbrella group," although it may never actually come together as a group, represents influential contacts in the business environment that can help "keep the rain off the parade" by being a weather vane for the change effort and heading off premature negative reactions.

People may show up in more than one location on the network if they are playing multiple roles, sometimes squeezing them in a conflict of interest, complicating the work of the stewards of change. For example:

- Senior executives providing strategic business guidance for the whole organization are often also leaders of sometimes competitive internal business units targeted for change.

- People from the evolving organization will play roles on analysis, design, and planning teams, sometimes supporting change in things "near and dear" to their colleagues back home.

- Experts providing process strategy guidance may also be resources for possible developmental support that could significantly increase their personal reward if incorporated into the effort.

- People from the evolving organization may also be members of influential networks in the organization's business environment that are threatened by the change underway.

Where specific people show up in your network depends on the roles they are playing, not necessarily where they come from in your present organizational structure.

Communication Strategy

Your communication strategy has to provide guidance to the players in the change role network for developing specific communication plans and conducting activities. A good communication strategy will promote understanding, support, and involvement in the change effort. It will provide for a listening environment for continually improving the direction, design decisions, and ultimate implementation of the changes. The strategy must provide clear responsibilities and support roles for communication and facilitate planning that will cover objectives, content, media, mechanisms, and scheduling of communication activities. Establishing the strategy will allow for stewardship of the overall communications pattern to help promote consistency of messages and information, assure ready access to sources and updated content, and promote network members taking ownership of the continuous improvement of the processes and of materials.

We talk with clients about three kinds of communication for their strategies: teach/tell, listen/learn, and dialogue and engagement. Understanding the distinctions can help you with your communication strategy and clarify your objective and media choices. The terms mean different things to different people and different authorities, but for our work we use them in the following context. *Teach/tell* fits when you have information that you want to put out that can be sufficiently "codified" (put into linear verbal or written expression without losing significant meaning). *Listen/learn* handles the same kind of information from the other end, when you have an information gap you want to close. *Dialogue* is a two-way interactive process; the objective of the exchange is the transfer of knowledge and meaning that cannot be easily codified or the development of new knowledge and meaning from the exchange and interplay of the information from the parties. *Engagement* moves from dialogue into applying the knowledge and meaning for joint decisions and action in the lives and worlds of the parties. In practice, communications cannot always be cleanly classified, but the distinctions can help in turning your communication strategy into specific communication plans. Keep in mind that, during a change process, people most always carry the same five questions with them:

1. "What is happening?"
2. "Why is it happening?"
3. "When is it happening?"
4. "How will I be impacted [by the outcomes and in the process]?"
5. "Where can I go with questions, issues, and concerns?"

In this arena of communications in a change situation, you really have your work cut out for you. Communications are about more than just the exchange of information. They are also about relationships, upon which change work is built. Communications always convey a combination of thoughts, feelings, and images of the players. There is always conscious and unconscious content. There is always filtering, both outgoing and incoming. There is always distortion by the media. There is always noise in the messages and the environment through which they travel (see Figure 2.2).

It's more of a wonder that we can ever understand each other at all than a wonder that we don't always understand one another. Misunderstandings in communication can seriously undermine the relationships your network needs in order to do its work well. So whatever your communication intention, include some means for checking out what the parties have heard and what that meant to them.

To close out this piece of the discussion, we include some welcome advice from a colleague, Marsh Clegg (2000). Marsh was the lead internal change steward in the high-performance redesign of a major marine transportation company that we supported. He is now working with us in developing the communication strategy of a large information technology and business process change effort with a different company.

Marsh advises that in putting together your communication strategy and plans, consider leveraging off of existing channels of communication when possible, because people work best with the familiar. Then help support application of the strategy and exercise of the network by providing for tools, training, and content development support to network members. You want to set conditions by which everyone has the opportunity to become engaged as communicators and potential change leaders, and you want to enroll others in communication planning and accomplishment. You want to make listening and initiating contact a universal responsibility. You want people to be proactive in staying linked and integrated with other people's initiatives. And you want to build the habit and processes for people to come together easily and quickly to get help and support, to establish and update plans, and to coordinate actions during all the stages of the change process. And, especially in

Figure 2.2. The Art of Communication.

Intended Message	Filters		Filters	Received Message
• Thoughts • Feelings • Self-Image	• Beliefs about the other • Context of the message • Communication pattern • Knowledge • Beliefs, attitudes, and values in general • Feelings • Personal agendas • Language • Culture	Media Distortion Noise	• Beliefs about the other • Context of the message • Communication pattern • Knowledge • Beliefs, attitudes, and values in general • Feelings • Personal agendas • Language • Culture	• Thoughts • Feelings • Impressions

"I know you think you heard what you thought I said, but I'm not sure I said what I really meant."

the early phases of a change process, include the following considerations in all of your communication plans:

- Whatever the topic, address or be prepared to include answers to the following *top five questions on everyone's mind in a change situation*.

    What is happening?

    Why is it happening?

    When will it happen?

    How will it affect me?

    How will people be involved and how can they find additional information?

- Repeat the "elevator message" of the business case and vision for the future (a short, succinct message you could put out between stops of an elevator).

- Insist that your own listening take precedence over telling.

- Give priority to dialogue.

- Use multiple mediums for critical teach/tell information.

- Clearly identify the objectives for each communication activity.

- Check frequently for alignment of objectives and the productivity of the process for the parties in a communication activity.

- Keep an open process, and test for what people heard.

- Actively respond to feedback by deepening your understanding through listen/learn, rather than first reacting with teach/tell.

Don't underestimate the need to repeat the message (vision), even when you "know" everyone has heard it time and again. Even with your best efforts, there will be many who won't remember why you're changing the organization. A colleague, who once led a large-scale organizational redesign for a mid-size business, often recalls a case in point. With a provisional design in place, and months of involving employees in the design and implementation, he held one of a series of employee Q&A sessions to communicate the next steps. At that time a senior vice president asked, with a straight face, "Why are we reorganizing?" Although this got a few chuckles from several employees, the question was taken seriously and led to a rather thorough discussion of the "why's" that had not surfaced before.

To clarify the effort required to keep communications moving, take a moment to think about who has to be able to answer those five questions regarding the change. Use Exhibit 2.1 to document your plan.

Developing a Dialogue About the State of the Business

The next piece of work is to use your communication strategy to begin a dialogue around the state of the business and its major processes. In Task I you developed a great deal of information about the state of your work system; now it is time to take it on the road. No matter how collaborative and inclusive you may have tried to be in Task I, there is inevitably a wider audience to include as you strive for an alignment of sentiment about the needs, direction, and strategy for change that will support Tasks III and IV ahead—evoking change leadership and expanding understanding and commitment within the organization. Use your communications network to figure out who this next audience ought to be. Use your communication strategy to figure out how to involve them.

This work of raising awareness begins to build a common ground from which to start creative thinking. The dialogue component

Exhibit 2.1. Communication Plan for the Change Effort.

Communication Network:	Primary Responsibility:
Stakeholder:	Support:

Activity	Objective	Schedule	Target	Program Support

here is critical. As you begin to talk about the current state, there are a number of reactions that occur inside the organization. Recognize that the business came to be where it is because people were doing what they thought to be best—or at least correct. The current system is a result of the best thinking of the past. One of the first reactions that emerges in many large organizations is defensiveness. A common error is to take the current state and bludgeon the organization with the data, highlighting all of the errors and negative outcomes. This will result in immediate reactions from the organization's members, but they will usually be reactions that either move them into short-term problem solving, defensive withdrawal from the change process, or offensive attack on it.

A common leadership style emphasizes the problems of the organization. In the 1960s it was named "management by exception." The dissatisfied leader who drives for better performance through calling out what cannot be tolerated usually creates lots of motion, but often little in cohesive movement toward focused change. The scolding finger (whether intentionally shaken or not) tends to divert attention away from the message toward the deliverer of the message. This optimizes itself in light of the problems, rather than to come together to optimize the whole.

The amount of time spent on this work can vary greatly. You can go back to the change equation for guidance, but don't get caught up in non-helpful, lengthy reanalysis of the information. What you want is to stress the urgency of the situation and give the people "good data" from which to form their own judgments. You don't want to mince the truth, but you also don't want to undermine their sense of pride in who they are and what they have done.

You also want to steer toward common stakes the people share so the players won't be tempted to set themselves against each other in a game of blame and hide. However, you will have to tailor the details to the audience. An organization that has many different locations and strong functional divisions may not even have a common view of what the major business processes are. Think of how a sales group and an associated manufacturing group can have a very different set of expectations for success, different issues, and different enabling processes. The process of coming together around a few central themes and how they are working can take a great deal of patience and understanding from the people involved. Doing this can take a good deal of artful planning and execution on the part of the change stewards. The work is worthwhile, however, because you're helping everyone pack up and move to the same starting point for the journey ahead.

Developing a Dialogue About the Business Case for Change

Deciding whether or not change is worthwhile is a closely related but different piece of work. In terms of the change equation, the dialogue looks more at dissatisfaction with the status quo and gives people the opportunity to come to peace with that. On the other hand, the business case explores the relative costs of doing or not doing something about it. If the different objectives merge too much, many people smell a sales job. They suspect a strategically manipulative purpose behind the invitation for discussion. They say, "If you have already made up your mind, why did you bother to ask my opinion?" However, no matter how you frame it, the case for change will usually have already come up in the dialogue around the current state. Some people look at a situation and see what is, while others look at a situation and see what should be. If you want honest dialogue, people have to be free to address what's on page one for them. Keeping the two issues sufficiently separate requires artful facilitation.

If you have already made up your mind about changing, we suggest you reverse the order of these two pieces of work. Give people the business case, then give them the data that you used to frame it, and then ask for disagreement or validation of what you propose. If it is honest data and they still reach a different conclusion, you can open up the wanted dialogue about how and why each of you sees it so differently. After all, it's the dialogue and the exchange of meaning that you require for the tasks ahead. The specifics of the content at any one time don't matter as long as it is relevant and heading you toward eventually building common ground.

Learning About Alternatives

Building on the understandings of the current state and the business-based case for change, the next step is to explore creative ways out of your situation. The exploration should be both broad and deep. There will already be good thoughts about possibilities for change that have never been taken seriously or that have come from sources not taken very seriously by the decision makers in the organization. Find ways to take a deeper look at some of the potential of these homegrown ideas.

At the same time, look broadly across your industry and others for creative divergence. Establish a "learning community" within your organization. Find people who would relish the work and be open to new ideas but who are still practical enough to be credible to the population as a whole. Work with them to develop a core value for expanding thinking and widening the possibility for the future. Their primary work is bringing ideas back to the organization, not just convincing themselves of the best ways to go. This is a major trip point. It is easy for even good, solid folks to get so far into the adventure that they leave their colleagues too far behind. Help them develop their ability to use the communication strategy and relate person-to-person with the organization. The first task for this community is to learn how to work together to seek out, learn about, and evaluate different ideas and concepts as a group. They can start by establishing an initial set of areas to explore and by deciding which areas to go into first, planning what each person is going to do or look for, taking the first few steps, critiquing the results, discussing what they did well and what they missed, then moving on to plan the next bit of the task. It is tempting, in the name of efficiency, to lay it all out for people. However, this will rob them of the need, and chance, to really engage the job. Another trip point is encouraging them to do it all—plan their approach, collect their information, frame their position, and make their report—in one big cycle. People have been doing that in organizations for decades without much happening. Help them get into this building process in which they take their colleagues along with them.

Education is a good place to start. Attend sessions with the goal of learning enough about relevant technology or process to discuss their particular limits and possibilities with others in the community. Target public sessions that are not limited to your industry. Draw parallels with what you are doing in your business and explore new uses for the ideas. Take the opportunity to learn from others in sessions as well as from the subject-matter experts who are making presentations. Look for networking opportunities to expand contacts for your learning community.

Take the time to read trade publications as well as general literature in the field. There are opportunities to learn from what other industries are doing, as well as to discover emerging trends and technologies. Sprinkle this reading with personal development and growth. People in all parts of the world have been puzzling over change for centuries and have written extensively about it.

Attend conferences with other members from your organization. Divide yourselves across the conference and see how many connections you can make. There is a wealth of information freely shared in conferences, through keynote speakers, industry presenters, and interesting participants. Come together to process learnings and evaluate your progress during the course of the conference.

Arrange presentations from consultants, others in the industry, people from other industries, academics, community leaders, or futurists. Schedule time to have discussions with these people about what you are hearing and the questions being raised for you. Take the time to listen to what others already know. Use this time to explore, discuss, and look for trends in your thinking.

Another powerful learning is to make site visits to other industries or businesses. This is not benchmarking or sharing of best practices, but searching for how other organizations are different. Look for sites that have an interesting difference or that have some attribute that particularly intrigues you. You are looking for what is different, challenges they have faced, what they have learned from their own journey.

All of this can be very heady and exciting, but it will be of minimal value if the community members don't bring their colleagues, who are back in the day-to-day business of the organization, along with them. Work hard with them to use the communication strategy and to bring their excitement to others in the organization.

Developing a Compelling Vision for the Future

A vision is not a mission. A mission is a sense of purpose in an environment. A vision is what it will look and feel like in that environment when you have achieved your mission. Begin by imagining an ideal future without regard to how difficult or practical it may be. Really get in touch with it; experience its look, feel, and sounds. Pull a group together to start—people who have been pitching in so far. Build a collective list of common characteristics from the stories you each are creating. Take these out to others and ask for their input. Find out if there are others who see that vision as a viable future, something they could get behind.

A vision is something that lives within people, not a few words on a piece of paper. Find a way to have the people build it, rather than search for a senior manager to put "his" or "her" vision into a statement for the organization. Vision statements developed this way are often seen as just another criticism by the people. Visioning can be hard work, but it can also be fun, energizing, and productive in a large-group setting. Bunker and Alban (1997) have excellent recommendations. Eventually, every member of the organization will have to find compelling meaning in the vision himself or herself.

Developing a Strategy and Proposed Approach to Change

There are four aspects to consider when you formulate a strategic approach to the change effort you are facing. One is the estimated scope and impact of the potential changes discussed in Chapter One. The second relates to how clear you can be about your desired end state and how to get there. The third is how much inclination and tolerance the organization has to explore its sense of purpose deeply. The fourth has to do with your position on how open and participative to be in your work with the Ten Tasks.

Clarity About Your Desired End State and How to Get There. The four-pane window shown in Figure 2.3 represents four very different change situations. The titles in parentheses in each pane represent the "best fit" approach to each situation. Your strategy and approach to the Ten Tasks will depend in part on which quadrant your change situation fits.

The more you move clockwise from straightforward strategic and business planning through project management, action research, and discovery learning, the more interactive, creative, and flexible

Figure 2.3. The Change Window.

	Know How to Get There	Don't Know How to Get There
Know the End State	II. Development Program *(Project Management)*	III. Planned Change *(Action Research)*
Don't Know the End State	I. Strategic and Business Planning *(Business Process)*	IV. Transformational Change *(Discovery Learning)*

you will have to be in your application of the Ten Tasks. The more you move counterclockwise from a transformational change situation to straightforward strategic and business planning, the more the application of the Ten Tasks becomes straightforward action planning that can be systematically managed to clear objectives. One danger is that the comfort of the structure present in quadrants I and II, or the pressure of time and expense within the organization, or the certainty of change stewards about the change can lead to approaches that are much more mechanistic than the situation really calls for.

At the early phase of a change, it may not be clear what will be coming up in the change process. You may not really know how complex or deep the organizational impact of business process changes targeted in Task I will be until you move into the process analysis of Task V. You can continuously update your judgments about the organization's readiness and past experience with change begun in Task I, but you will not know its real capacity until you get into it in Task VII and Task IX. For example, in an information technology driven change, if systems analysis in Task V shows that apparent changes will mainly amount to a different look and feel for hands-on users, no matter how costly, difficult, and sophisticated the changes to the electronics might be, there won't be much organizational impact. Taking a solid project management approach to the overall effort will suffice. If the technology changes drive more fundamental business process reinvention too, then the overall business process redesign and implementation planning efforts have to extend out from project management to include stakeholder collaboration in the planning of change. If the possibilities surfaced by the technology design options encountered in Tasks V and VI create "demand pull" from the stakeholder for even more significant business improvements, you are edging into the collaborative learning realm of transformational change.

The Depth of the Organization's Search for Its Purpose. Assessing an organization's purpose might seem like an unnecessary task, one for which the result would be obvious. However, different people, departments, or functions may have different ideas about what the organization's purpose is. Also, some members of the organization may be unwilling to spend time exploring what they feel is an obvious issue. However, the organization's purpose will shape any necessary changes, so all those involved must be in agreement. The willingness of the participants to probe their reason for being, the questions you ask, and the nature of the data obtained all have a great impact on the nature of the case for change.

To illustrate the level to which purpose can be explored, think about reviewing your personal finances. A formal accounting would include cash balances, portfolio holdings, property, liabilities, and so forth. Doing an "as is" assessment could simply require a balance sheet or a net worth calculation. With this, there are a number of possible actions that might ensue. Looking at the data could lead you to make a number of evaluative judgments, such as: "My cash is too low; I need to reduce expenses," "My cash is too high; I need to increase investments," or "I'm paying too much in taxes; I need advice from my CPA." All of these tend to move in a problem-solving direction.

A more complete review would include financial goals and intentions: "Where do I want to be in five years? In ten years?" "How much will I need to pay for college?" "When will I retire?" The comparison of the static balance sheet with a goal or direction becomes an intention-based review. There may be significant differences in the action that comes from this review.

Another level of difference is to provide the reflective part of the review: "Why do I own this particular portfolio?" "What sort of investment strategy did I have?" "Did it work?" "What sort of decisions was I making?" "What sort of data was I considering?" "If I was paying insufficient attention to this, where was my attention focused instead?" "Am I comfortable with the choices I made over time?" "How did I do?"

Of these three scenarios, the first is the most straightforward and drives the most transactional change. The decisions are based mostly on data summations and tend to be based more on "business rules." In this example, the balances might be compared to a standard or guideline, such as number of months' income held in cash, percentage of portfolio in securities, or debt-to-income ratio.

The second scenario requires a greater focus on your intentions and moves more into strategic planning. It requires a deeper search into your values and principles and examining the bases of your priorities.

The third scenario is the most reflective and, because of this, the most sensitive to explore. It opens questions of choice and the reality that you have chosen the principle by which you live. However, they are not written in stone. This much exploration of the possibilities in a situation can be exciting, but also frightening and confusing for the individual.

The same three levels exist in organization change, from problem solving to redesign to self-renewal. The task for change stewardship is not only to help with good logical approaches to the different analysis and decision requirements, but also to help the population deal appropriately with the anxieties connected to each requirement.

Your Position on Participation. There are many approaches to involving the targets of change in the process of analysis, design, and implementation. Each is based on different sets of beliefs about people and theories about human psychology. Some of these theories picture people as the sum of the random engagements in their lives and the consequences they experienced as a result of their behavior in those experiences. Other theories say that instinctive or acquired needs drive human behaviors. Still others take the stand that people are driven by their unconscious or beyond. Probably all of these propositions are in some part true. However, the Ten Tasks are based on a belief that it is most productive to approach people as intentional, learning, self-actualizing beings who engage life in a meaningful way according to their purposes and what they have learned so far. Therefore, what you see in this book has a strong bias toward a collaborative "learning" approach.

Because organization change addresses reconfiguring a complex, living work system, not just a single, inanimate object such as a statue, collective agreement on the intent and design is as important as the creative act itself. Because a creative act is very personal and individual, designing work system means bringing individual creativity to collective consensus. This fact drives many change leaders to abandon participative involvement in design because they worry that they can never achieve a consensus except in a small, relatively controllable group. This is particularly true when your analysis of the four complexity slopes in Task I (changes in the business, the technical system, the human organization, and the people) shows the impact of the potential change pretty far up those slopes. We take the opposite position. You may be able to save time in the process of agreeing on a conceptual design by limiting the participation, but eventually you will end up spending that time (and maybe more) getting everyone to buy in to the design.

Viewing participation as the beginning of implementation has another unexpected benefit. For example, leadership in one company was frustrated by the lengthy timetable for design and implementation. They had seen other divisions accomplish reorganizations in just months. The timetable for this change was six to nine months, and senior management felt "embarrassed" by the extended period and was placing pressure on the design team to accelerate its effort. When it was explained that implementation had already begun after the first few employee workshops, everyone relaxed and enthusiastically supported the effort.

Figure 2.4 represents the tradeoffs you make as you move from small design team models to full participation models for even the most complex and in-depth changes. As the figure shows, the farther you move toward full participation for work system design, the higher the required readiness for change and the shorter the overall time for completion. With the participative approaches, less detail is available up-front because of the number of people involved in design decisions. However, the detail doesn't have to be defined

Figure 2.4. Participation Options.

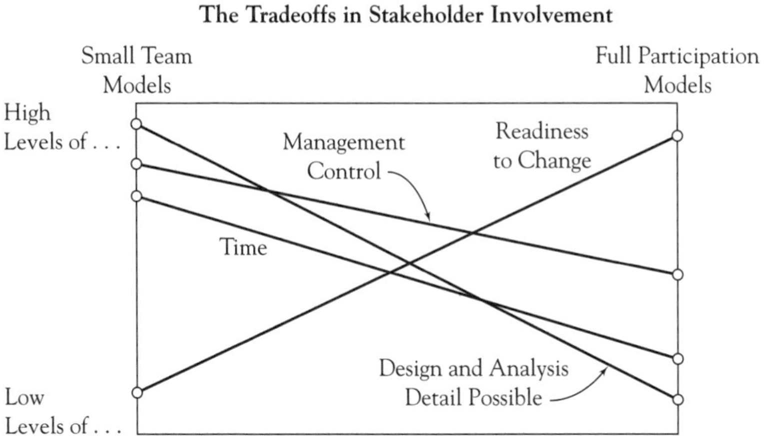

The Tradeoffs in Stakeholder Involvement

yet. During implementation, the actual people who are responsible for making the real system work will be coming to agreement on the critical specifications. The slope of the management control line represents a loss of ability to be arbitrary in design and implementation decisions. The greater the number of people involved, the more soundly thought out and discussed decisions must be in order to get everyone on board. The fear of loss of control, however, often leads managers to abandon sponsorship of change processes that may be a little noisy but are working quite well for the comfort of quieter approaches for which they don't have to put quite so much faith in the people.

We have no prescriptions for you to follow in pulling together your strategy for changing, beyond calling your attention to the issues we have just addressed. You are too unique, your change situation is too unique, and the character of your organization and its environment is too unique for "patent medicine." You will have to use your best judgment, in collaboration with others, and be ready to change your choices to match the circumstances as the change unfolds. Whatever you decide is the right approach for the organization, you have to assume that your own change stewardship is in quadrant four, transformational change, and take a discovery learning approach to your own decision, development, and personal growth.

Developing a High-Level Action Plan

Develop a high-level action plan that follows your strategy and proposed approach to changing. This should be just enough so that you can answer the question, "How will this work move forward?" Use your best judgment to create an overall time frame and identify the main phases; the detail will have to come later. This plan should include the major known resource requirements for each phase. It should also detail the level of stakeholder engagement that is desired to move forward with the change. Expect expanding levels of involvement throughout the engagement. It is easy to underestimate the amount of effort required to engage a large number of people who are dispersed across wide areas. You don't need anything special to do this; use your organization's planning and estimating experts and processes to help you. Ultimately this will all have to work its way into your company's business planning process. Involve stakeholders as much as practical. The sooner you can get those people at the table doing that planning in support of the change, the faster and easier change will occur. Always remember that the ultimate responsibility of change, of preparing for it and carrying it through implementation, is in the receiving organization.

Implementing an Infrastructure

Develop an infrastructure of people whose work it will be to manage the rest of the change effort. This group should be representative of the larger system and have the resources and authority to engage the rest of the organization. These people should collectively have knowledge of all parts of the organization and the particular issues relevant in each. They should have credibility in their own organizations and with the leadership of the overall organization.

Most importantly, they should support the vision and want to do the work.

Apply the information and principles of this book to plan and establish this infrastructure. It may be formal or virtual, but if you apply what you are learning here, it will work for you. Aim to imitate the cultural vision for the future of the changing organization when you set up how this infrastructure will work. If you would like some good ideas and a set of questions you can use in establishing this infrastructure, refer to Chapter Nine. The same ideas presented there about transitioning to a new organizational work unit design apply to forming the infrastructure that will guide the accomplishment of the Ten Tasks.

Summary

The work of Task II has put into motion the process that will create and sustain change in your organization. As stated earlier, the Ten Tasks emphasize the organizational skills of planning work and working plans. Bringing the people in your organization together to engage the business case for change and to agree on a desirable future begins to increase the readiness of the organization to move in a new direction.

Points to Remember

Plan Your Communications and Engagement Work. This critical step is the mechanism that will drive change in the organization.

Use a Dialogue Process. Always approach your engagements with the intention of learning and growing together.

Seek Learning from Outside and Share Broadly. Look to the outside work for possibilities. Share the information through the communication network to stimulate thinking and create alternatives for the organization.

Be Clear About the Type of Change You Are Considering. Use the "change window" to become clear about what you are considering. Plan your engagement and work according to the approach required in each quadrant.

———————

Common Trip Points

Criticizing the Current State. A common reaction among executives who see poor results is to criticize the organization immediately. This can derail potentially powerful change efforts by driving early reactive change or by heightening the defense mechanisms of the organization.

Ignoring the Current State. There is often a tendency to skip over the assessment of the current state with the well-intentioned belief that it is better to focus purely on the future. The time spent dealing with the current state brings people to a common place for designing the future. It validates the past and creates early agreements in the organization.

Imitating Others. Learning about what other organizations are doing can create a certain amount of "me too"-ism. The work associated with looking at others is in deciding whether or not a given solution or practice fits your organization and how you might reach a similar point.

Seeing the Task as Linear. This process is nonlinear and requires that the outputs from each engagement be fed into the next deliberation. Don't try to do all the engagement in one cycle! Only through repeatedly engaging the members of the organization through dialogue and deliberation can a shared vision emerge.

Setting the Vision Too Soon. When the work of creating the compelling vision for the future begins to proceed, it is easy to lose patience and move quickly to what seems at the time to be a good choice. Stay in creative suspense long enough to run trial visions across segments of the organization, and be flexible enough to alter the vision as a result of the learning process.

Vision Shared vs. Shared Vision. There is often a tendency to resort to traditional methods of deployment by taking a vision for the future to the organization's leadership, who then endorse it and announce it as where the organization is going. Leadership's endorsement is required and critical, but sharing a vision does not create a shared vision.

Seeing the Process as Slow. One of the seeming paradoxes of working through this task is that, although the processes of dialogue and engagement seem to be glacially slow, the process of change and creating strategic alignment is incredibly fast. As soon as the critical mass moves into alignment, change often begins to unfold in unexpected and unanticipated ways. The infrastructure that works to enable the process must be fluid and adaptable, as the organization can quickly move past the ability of a small group to stay ahead of it.

Treating Transformational Change as Transactional. True transformational change requires many role shifts, thought shifts, and action shifts. These cannot be identified before the change and must be worked through with the people during the change process. This kind of uncertainty is not accommodated very well by good traditional project management approaches that begin with clear specifications and detailed planning of the work ahead (a transactional change situation). A common error is to attempt to diminish the discomfort with the uncertainty by trying to utilize project management methodologies that set unrealistic expectations and provide little real guidance for change activities.

Involving Too Few People on Too Small a Task. Change ultimately involves *every member* of an organization. If you think that you can approach change without everyone ultimately getting on board, you are kidding yourself. Many change efforts use input sessions or small tasks in the change as a way of "involving" the people of the organization. The only real way to be involved in change is by rolling up your sleeves and getting to work. The sooner you can get everyone doing that, the better off you will be.

3

Task III: Evoking Change Leadership

"When the going gets tough, the tough get . . .
together!"

In the uncertainties of a change process, people don't hang onto concepts, they hang onto people. They don't just look for safe harbor in the storm, they look for the comfort of other boats safe in a harbor. When change puts its heaviest strain on the fiber of our relationships, the relationships that are the strongest will determine the direction in which the organization is pulled. When the path ahead is uncertain, people don't look for somebody to follow, they look for leaders they trust and will follow them almost anywhere. Task III is about searching out and evoking this kind of leadership for the change ahead.

The Work of Task III

The work of Tasks I and II serves to clarify and establish the organization's new direction and increase energy to move toward that vision. By this time, it isn't a case of whether you're going, but a case of how—specifically—you will get there. There has been opportunity for the voices of difference to be heard and for the collective mind to be set. There will still be differences, opposition to the direction, and many people on the fence in a wait-and-see stance. But the die has been cast. It is now that evoking change leadership is critical. You must have change leadership that is aligned with the new vision, that will start the multitude thinking through what these changes mean to them, and that will begin developing behaviors to enable those changes. The outcome of this task is a network of leaders who are actively exploring "local visions" and working change throughout the organization.

"Leadership" in this book is not used in a strictly hierarchical sense. We use leadership far more comprehensively to describe those people who will begin creating the new organization. These people will be the front-runners in understanding the implications of the change and in thinking through how their work systems will be impacted. The work to flush out and get these leaders is the work of Task III, which includes:

- Establishing a leadership network

- Involving potential change leaders in exploring "local visions" that support the overall vision for the future

- Enabling the leadership network to act

- Providing support for leaders' future roles

- Defining change leadership behaviors for "walking the talk"

- Clearly defining the leadership rewards and consequences

- Identifying and securing the required support and resources for the work ahead.

Establishing a Leadership Network

At this point, members of the organization must begin to think through what these changes mean to them and to develop behaviors to enable them. Leadership at this time is critical. After the vision begins to crystallize, the next piece of work becomes preparing a critical mass of leadership that is aligned with the new vision and is prepared to begin "living out" the new system.

The Players in an Organizational Change

Some time ago, a valued colleague of ours, Gerry Miller, introduced us to the idea that there are three kinds of players in an organization change: sponsors, change agents, and targets (Miller, 1982, 1999). *Sponsors* are those who clearly want and initiate the change; *change agents* are those who will take the changes to the people; *targets* are the people whose work and work lives will be changed in the process. The roles aren't necessarily mutually exclusive. Sponsors and targets often act as change agents, change agents ultimately become sponsors if they stay the course, and everyone at some time feels, for better or worse, like a target. When we started in this work, people assumed that sponsors meant senior executives of the organization. Change agents was a euphemism for middle and front-line management, and targets were the masses who would have to put up with it. The collaborative spirit that grew out of the quality movement in the 1980s made it clearer to the members of organizations that sponsorship could come from anywhere; that change agents were enlisted, not assigned; and that being a target was a matter of adapting "best practices," not merely of being put upon. Of course, there were and are still poorly thought through and clumsily executed changes. We also understand that what's good for the many is not always good for the few. The Ten Tasks, however, is about making good choices, developing the right frameworks, and helping each of the players act out his or her role in the best interest of each of them and of the enterprise. To do their jobs well, people in each of the three roles must do the following:

- Sponsors must

    Be able to state the business case and vision clearly and succinctly

Have some personal investment in the effort

Set the standards and boundaries for the change

Walk the talk and demonstrate personal sacrifice in the process

Search out and support change agents

- Change agents must

    Answer the questions "What?" "When?" "Why?" and "How?"

    Work through the details of change interventions

    Walk the talk and demonstrate commitment to the process

    Be credible with the people

- Targets must

    Be able to picture themselves in the vision

    Understand the what, when, why, and how of the process

    Become proactively involved in the process

Leadership in a change effort is about helping these people find the value and the commitment to play their roles well.

The Jobs of "Bosses" During a Change Process

People with a formal leadership position in a traditionally hierarchical organization undergoing change will have more leverage for pulling it ahead or shutting it down than the average person on the front line. To be in the acceleration business, members of the executive team have to work at the following:

- Being a "team" related to the change, not remaining a loose confederation of different opinions

- Monitoring each other to make sure beliefs, words, and actions are in alignment

- Being visible, leading "learners" in the process

- Being excellent *sponsors*, active *change agents*, and model *targets*

- Sanctioning the process, allocating resources, and making sure there is someone taking care of the work

- Making sure the approach taken fits the change situation and the potential impact of the changes

- Making sure the change leadership network is alive and well

- Providing ongoing strategic business guidance to the change effort

- Staying in touch and communicating, communicating, communicating

As a middle or front-line manager in a change, you must do the following:

- Become engaged enough to influence good decisions in the process and support the decisions once they are made, even if they aren't your "first choice"

- Make these "your" changes, not "their" changes

- Be able to state the business case and vision clearly and succinctly

- Work with your leadership groups and your peers to be a "team" related to the change, rather than remain a loose confederation of different opinions

- Actively seek feedback to be sure that what you say is what you believe and that what you do matches what you say

- Be a visible, leading "learner" in the process

- "Sanction" the process within your organization, allocate the needed resources, and make sure there is somebody taking care of the change work that has to be done

- Stay in touch with your people related to the changes and communicate, communicate, communicate

- Show that you also have some personal investment in the effort

- Work actively to set the standards and boundaries for the change in your organization

- Search out and support change leaders in your organization

Identifying the Leadership in Your Organization

Identifying the leadership of the organization requires looking for formal and informal influence both inside and outside the organization. It is important to understand that the expectation for these leaders is to change their own actions, not to change the actions of others. Often the leadership is in nonhierarchical authority positions. Technical advisors, process operators, sales advisors, and trainers often provide significant informal leadership to the organization. Identify these leaders and how they influence the organization. People from the outside of the organization can also provide a force to move the organization toward the vision for the future. For instance, customers can provide a continual source of leadership when they are enrolled and committed to the vision. Community figures can often significantly influence behavior as well as beliefs and attitudes of members of the organization. In union environments, local leadership may have to extend into the larger union governance system. In strongly regulated environments, significant changes may require looking to the regulatory agency to identify leaders. Think through the influence exerted on your organization by people outside and inside. Use this as a collaborative exercise to open engagement dialogues. Use Exhibit 3.1 to document your findings.

It is useful to consider the number of leaders who will be required. The size of the leadership network will have to be a significant portion of the entire organization. An initial target of 10 percent is a good rule of thumb. A very complex organization can require many more. To determine the appropriate number of leaders, think in terms of the overall organization and how it actually functions.

- How geographically dispersed is the organization?

- How different is the organization functionally?

- Are there different business units?

- Are there different technical processes?

- Are there different customer bases?

- Are there significant cultural differences?

For each of the significant differences, consider what sort of local leadership will best support adaptability. Each leader will provide a point of deliberation for the small decisions that are made on a daily basis. Identifying where these deliberation processes take place is a way to identify the local leadership. This is a good time to check these assumptions with people inside the organization. Use Exhibit 3.2 to think through this network. Also refer to Exhibit 3.1 to stimulate your ideas.

Exhibit 3.1. Identifying Sources of Influence.

Proposed Change:		Primary Responsibility:	
		Support:	

Person or Group Exerting Influence	Type of Influence	On Whom	How Is the Influence Manifested?	Engagement Plan
Customers				
Suppliers				
Support Organizations				
Regulators				
Internal to the System				

Exhibit 3.2. Planning a Leadership Network.

Proposed Change:		Primary Responsibility:
Organization:		Support:

Work or Organization Unit	Type of Leadership Requirements	Potential Network Member	Type of Support Required	Engagement Plan

Another point to consider with this group is how it will function. Often, large change efforts are driven and supported by special teams who come together to plan and enable the overall change effort. Members of the leadership network will not necessarily be full-time members of that team. The leadership network members do, however, have to be full-time functioning members of the organization. Leaders in the network will continue to do their ongoing work while taking on additional responsibilities. This will require extra work, effort, and time on their part.

Because these people still operate in the larger organization, becoming a part of the leadership network will pose some difficulty and even risk to them. Going outside the hierarchy and formal lines of the organization can create situations in which these people will be operating at odds with management or even their peers. Ideally, members of the leadership network will participate because (1) they are willing to do so, (2) they have some passion to create positive changes in the organization, and (3) they are sponsored for the activities they are about to pursue. Sponsors must ensure that leaders have the resources required to participate. Sponsors must also ensure that leaders can operate publicly in their role. It is a big mistake to attempt to operate clandestinely. The people with whom leaders interface must be made aware that those in the leadership network will have a special role for some time to come.

The overall change leadership may have to negotiate with the members of the larger organization. The negotiation process itself serves as an intervention. The effort to enroll change leaders must model the level of participation expected for the overall effort. Going out to the larger organization and naming local leadership would not be consistent with a participative approach. Rather than identifying local leadership yourself, open the question to the organization (or each part of the organization) and then enter the deliberation process locally. This will serve to model desired behavior and will help to develop the organizational competency required for making participative decisions.

Involving Potential Change Leaders

It is critical to involve local leaders in the creation of the future state. This is the first phase of moving an idea into actualization. Large-group processes are particularly useful at this point. Bring the members of the leadership network into the same room and begin the deliberation process early enough in the overall effort to ensure that there is still space to modify, clarify, or even amend the existing future state. A common error is to view this as a deployment or proclamation time, informing people of the changes to occur. On the contrary, the members of the leadership network should be viewed as a creative body whose work is as much to decide the organization's direction as it is to enable it.

Deepen Their Appreciation of Both Current and Future States

All change involves a creative tension between the current and future states. The existing business case for change should be expanded at this point, with the leadership extending the case down to the local level. A common error at this point is to build a business case for change at the macro level, create the vision for the future, and then move to deploy based on the future state only. Instead, to fully engage change, every member of the organization must evaluate the changes based on his or her own perception of the benefit of that change relative to his or her experience of the current state. The leadership network members will likely be ahead of the thinking of the rest of the organization and will thus have less support to engage the future state at this point. This increases the need for them to become thoroughly grounded in both the vision and in the current state.

Members of the leadership network may need to spend time in their work units gathering data to develop the local business case for change. This could be as simple as examining existing data or as complex as running engagement and assessment processes at each work location. The data must be comprehensive and relevant to the needs of that particular organization.

Generate Possibilities and Alternatives for the Local Visions

Members of the leadership network begin thinking about possibilities for their work unit. While it is reasonable to expect that those selected will have ideas about how the vision can be appropriate for their work system, there is an opportunity here to expand their thinking. This is a good time to give the leaders a fresh perspective that may be significantly different from what they have experienced. Take the time to put the leaders in touch with different work systems, with the expectation that they will simply learn and look nonjudgmentally at how others operate. This is often thought of as sharing best practices or benchmarking. Both of these processes are valuable in finding incremental improvements. However, to accomplish radical shifts, leaders must look at areas that are totally different. Go outside the business or even the industry. Look at other operating practices, using a different set of questions than you would use for benchmarking. Evaluate successful and unsuccessful businesses. Attempt to understand what makes those systems work or not work. This can be difficult because we often don't know the questions to ask, particularly in organizations that have significantly different operating principles. The key is to create a larger field of possibilities, rather than try to find a specific answer.

You may recall that, earlier in the process, the learning community used this method to generate possibilities for an overall vision for the organization. Here, the leadership network is generating local visions. This is a good example of the iterative nature of large-scale change.

It may be useful at this point to use a facilitator to guide the questioning and learning process. It is common to find the leaders with far more questions than when they started. They need to make sense of what they see. Using facilitation, you can stay focused on working through what you don't understand. Significant learning often comes from working out *why* you don't understand. This calls up belief sets and operating paradigms that are deeply rooted in the current state. These may be leading indicators of the work to come and can be the seeds of resistance in the larger organization. Develop the knowledge and awareness of these paradigms within the leadership network and equip network members to follow the same process with others. It is important that this group understand the learning process involved in change so that they can support it.

Clarify and Solidify the Local Visions

The local leadership has to integrate its vision for the future into a clear picture of what will be substantially different. This will be unique to each organization. This local vision is a supplement to the overall vision that embodies the larger direction and provides guidance to the other members of the organization. The local network has two basic components: the overall vision and the local vision. These local elements create the first level of engagement and alignment with the larger work system. The elements must be developed in a manner consistent with the overall change effort. A common practice is to use an iterative process, creating the local visions in alignment with both the overall vision and the desired culture of the emerging workplace. It is important that this process be consistent with the overall spirit of change. For instance, think about the impact on the organization of bringing one hundred local leaders together to create an overall vision for the organization and then having those leaders develop local visions without involving members of their own work groups. Although the visions would be created, the message sent to the larger organization would be powerful and difficult to overcome later.

Another piece of this process is the individual leader's role and commitment to the effort. There is an individual component of how each leader will engage the system, what each will consider the most desirable elements of the future state, and how each will learn and grow through this effort. This has to be clarified at the individual level with the support of the leadership network. Having such a role in a large organization undergoing change can be a significant learning adventure and often results in career changes or life shifts. Providing adequate support for those who are in this role adds tremendous power both to the change effort and to the sustainability of the change. An organization's current capability for change is set by the last change undertaken. Good work enables not only one change to be made but all future changes as well.

Enabling the Leadership Network to Act

It has been said that an organization is always doing all that it can do—that many of the things represented in the future state literally cannot be done in the current organization. Limitations may be caused by poor technology or lack of resources, skills, or knowledge, insufficient performance support systems, or the habitual behaviors of the members of the organization. Often, the change leaders will understand the future state conceptually and believe in its benefits for the business, but will also understand that their personal roles will be significantly impacted and that their future in the system will be uncertain. Others may understand the change and benefits, but will have no idea how they would interact in the new system. This is common when the vision for the future includes significant differences in operating principles. An example of this is when organizations are moving to team systems. A local leader might truly desire the positive features of the team system, but recognize that (1) the current organizational rewards structure is designed to support individuals; (2) career paths in the current system are hierarchically determined; and (3) skills were developed for success in that system. The local leader might suddenly be ill-equipped to function in the new system. Another example would be technical experts who now commit significant energy outside their existing areas of expertise. They might wonder how they will provide leadership in an area in which they are not experts.

All of these questions are real for those moving into roles in the leadership network. To allay their fears, provide education in potential new roles and role requirements, career planning opportunities, and classes in managing personal change to liberate the members so they can begin the work of enabling change.

Providing Support for Leaders' Future Roles

The local leaders will live with one foot in the boat and one on the dock for some period of time. While they are working to create and enable the changes, they will also be completely entwined in the maintenance of the current state. The choices that they make, the actions that they take, and the counsel they offer to others in the organization will always be grounded in both the future state and the current state. Theirs is often an exhausting and thankless task. The risk is in being drawn completely back to the current state or status quo simply because they are immersed in it. When stress is high, the work load is increasing, and timelines are short, they will be more likely to operate by using automatic behaviors, all of which were learned in the current system (or worse, the previous system). The feedback they receive from within their organization will always be grounded in the current state, so it can be confusing and confrontational. It is necessary to provide a support network that operates from outside the current system to keep these folks centered and moving toward the future state.

The leadership network will have to have a mechanism for coming together as a community to provide support, share learning, and renew their commitment to the effort. Every group will have a unique timing requirement for this renewal work. Until the changes have been fully engaged by the organization, leaders must receive virtually all of their support from outside their work units. The network can provide a significant part of this support, but issues of timing and logistics may make it impractical for the network members to come together as a large group often enough to provide adequate support to one another. Also, in the early phases of the effort, the group may require a significant amount of external support simply to handle the group dynamics that emerge. This is a necessary piece of the change process, and it is critical to identify and secure the required external support and resources for change. The change leadership has to provide ongoing support for the leadership network both as a group and as individuals.

The growth and development of the members of the leadership network is an ongoing process. Treat this as a strategic element of the change effort and establish processes to handle it. The individuals in this network are often supported through coaching and mentoring. These are substantially different processes and serve different purposes.

Coaching is typically done through an individual learning contract with the change leaders. The goal of coaching should be to support the leaders' effort to sustain their new behaviors, clarify their thinking, and strengthen their reliance on the overall network. The change will be sustained through building internal relationships among change leaders, so coaching should address this goal.

Mentoring is typically an internal process, with the mentor being an internal expert in the system. Although mentoring is invaluable, remember that mentors will be offering advice and counsel based on their expertise in the *current* system. The best use of mentors at this point is as partners in puzzlement. Their deep understanding of the current system should be used to plan how to best engage that system in the change effort.

Defining Change Leadership Behaviors for "Walking the Talk"

The next piece of work for the leadership network is to define the behaviors required for them to "walk the talk." Some set of meaningful behaviors will clearly indicate the differences in the future state, a combination of business, technical, and interpersonal behaviors. At this time, these behaviors should be exhibited by the leadership network rather than demanded of the workforce at large.

These behaviors may be around involvement, supporting communications, or performing change-related activities. Some will be specific to the organization and its operations, such as changes in how mistakes are addressed. In general though, the network can be expected to exhibit behaviors that reflect how to do the "jobs" of sponsors, change agents, targets, and bosses in a change process.

Clearly Defining the Leadership Rewards and Consequences

After determining the behaviors expected from members of the leadership network, it is important to define the leadership rewards and consequences clearly. Ultimately, it is difficult for people to operate outside of the organizational reward structure for long periods of time. Large change efforts can place change agents at significant risk of falling out of the developmental path of the larger organization or of being overwhelmed by existing demands of the current state, with resulting consequences.

Identifying and Securing the Required Support and Resources

Although the initial support for change often comes from outside the system, sustaining it requires that there be support within the system after those resources leave. We recommend using as much internal support as is possible. Part of the task of local leadership is to create the support resources that the emerging organization will require. An error typical in change efforts is to underestimate the amount of resources required to completely integrate the future state. The downside to using internal resources is that supporting large-scale change requires some special expertise, which cannot always be quickly acquired. The up side (and our preferred position) is that, once developed, this internal expertise can expedite the change effort and provide greater sustainability.

The internal change and development support resources will not necessarily be the same people as the leadership network. The requirements for support resources, in terms of size and skills, are based on the local visions and the current understanding of the gap between the current and future states. The leadership network must be involved in setting the requirements for this group and in determining the way the group will interface with the organization as the change effort progresses. The internal resources must have the organizational capabilities and individual competencies to support the future state as it is defined at this point.

Summary

Task III can be thought of as constructing a leadership network. The network should engage all parts of the existing organization and serve as a link between those sponsoring the change, the change leadership, and the emerging work system. The individuals in the network will serve as beacons for the change and local integrators of the unique needs of all parts of the organization. Their work will be to carry the change down to the individual and support day-to-day efforts.

The identification, development, and support of this leadership network is an important and strategic step toward achieving the overall vision. Additionally, specific local visions must be created that are both relevant to the work unit and consistent with the overall vision. These local visions have to exist throughout the organization so that all parts of the organization are moving toward the overall vision. This network of leaders will also provide credible spokespersons to encourage the organization as a whole to support and nourish the future state.

The work of the network is to support the individual leaders in this critical work of change. It provides the information flow, as well as the skills, knowledge, and emotional support required.

Points to Remember

Establish Local Leadership for the Change Throughout the Organization. It is critical for all parts of the organization to have active and visible leadership for change. Take the time to identify leaders throughout the organization.

Provide an Opportunity for Each Leader to Frame His or Her Own Local Vision. Each leader, depending on his or her own career, interests, job position, and organizational interest, will have a unique spin on the overall vision. It is important for each leader to have the opportunity to create a vision of how his or her part of the organization will be decidedly different when the overall vision is achieved.

Common Trip Points

Too Much Dependence on Formal Hierarchy. The formal hierarchy's main purpose is to sustain the current state. Although you must honor its purpose and presence in a change effort, your efforts will be strongly challenged if you attempt to drive change while allowing the current state to be maintained.

Too Much Dependence on Formal Authority. It is critical that people who have formal authority in the organization be included in this step. However, that authority is not required to provide leadership. Look for leadership in all areas of the organization. Don't ignore the front-line employees. Credibility with others is just as important as credibility with leaders.

Too Small a Network. It often appears to be a daunting and expensive task to target 10 percent of your organization for a leadership network. Remember, everyone must get on board eventually. Time spent creating involvement now will accelerate the subsequent work of change tremendously.

Too Little Room for Local Vision. Every area must create a vision of its own corner of the organization. A rigid overarching vision will not allow people to make sense of it at their own level, which will slow down the process of gaining commitment and taking action to complete the change.

Task IV: Expanding Understanding and Commitment

Now that the organization has developed a fundamental description of the proposed change and the language to describe it, it is necessary to enable the organization to change. All organizations have the tendency to self-correct toward a known purpose. The pressures for self-correction come not only from within the organization, but from outside as well. Many stakeholders have vested interests in the existing outcomes and will quickly exert pressure to stop anything that they perceive might jeopardize the existing organization. These pressures, both inside and outside the organization, are often strong enough to stop change efforts in their tracks. Many approaches to change treat this natural reaction as resistance and use strategies to lessen, eliminate, or go around areas that might slow the change process.

Task IV of the Ten Tasks treats this "resistance" as a natural occurrence that is created by a widespread commitment to the current state. Even though members of the organization may understand and desire the vision for the future, moving toward that goal requires them to operate in some unknown or uncertain areas and may put stakeholders at significant personal risk. Task IV creates conditions whereby a broader group can understand the proposed change and become committed to attaining the new vision. Successful change requires that all members become more committed to the future vision than to the current state, even though all the organization's practices and norms are set in the current state.

The Work of Task IV

At this point, work with the organization and its immediate environment to establish a "safety zone" for beginning the transformation process and to start validating the change as "work" for the organization's membership. This requires that the most immediately active stakeholders in the environment and the members of the organization set up processes through which the conditions of the change and the conditions of the environment can be kept in constant touch. There are seven major components to this task:

- Establishing "safety nets" for the organization

- Establishing role structures for the change process

- Establishing widespread understanding of the change

- Beginning appropriate education processes for the entire organization

- Creating and supporting ongoing dialogue for the change process

- Using feedback systems

- Creating a more detailed action plan

Establishing Safety Nets for the Organization

In a high-wire act, the artists face a significant risk of falling. Safety nets are there to keep the results from being catastrophic. The net does *not* prevent them from falling. It simply assures that they have another chance to make the trip across. Change efforts often put people at risk—sometimes perceived, sometimes quite real. This element of risk can often be high enough that it prevents people from moving from wherever they currently are, even if the future is highly desirable.

Some approaches to change encourage change agents to "turn up the heat" and make members' current position so untenable that they have no choice but to move on at any cost. Although this works to move people, it does little to enroll them in long-term sustainable change and tends to consume a huge amount of their emotional and mental energy in the interim. The Ten Tasks build in the ability to change rapidly and intentionally, and it requires that all members of the organization use their energies to run their business productively and to create adaptive change at the same time. This requires lowering the perceived cost of the change at the individual level.

You must understand what people in the organization feel may happen to them. In some organizations, the risk may be loss of a current promotional path, loss of personal power, loss of a preferred role, or even loss of employment. People may fear being unable to perform in the new environment because of lack of skills or experience or they may worry about loss of personal relationships in the work group, about having to relocate, or about the unknown.

At another level, hesitation may simply be an indication of lack of clarity on how to proceed. Imagine that the organization is filled with people who are doing their best to run their business as it is today. They are committed to maintaining its integrity, meeting their customers' needs, and meeting their business objectives. It is not unusual to have a large number of people who are ready to make the change, who want the end result, but who see no path from here to there. For these people, setting out on an exploration of change often poses a significant threat to their current commitments.

For each of these cases, energy for change can be liberated by setting up safety nets. Granted, these nets do not eliminate risk (the high-wire artist can still fall); they simply reduce the negative consequence associated with it. Safety nets must be in multiple forms, based on what the people in the organization most need. The most important structure to have is whatever is most important to the people in the system.

Many common structural safety nets exist in today's organizations. These may take the form of resources for relocation, retraining, or re-skilling. These are all necessary for many of the possible outcomes of change. However, in times of great personal change and turbulence, most people draw their support from other people and from a sense of having some control over and choice in their lives. Often the greatest personal risk people perceive is having no control over their lives. One of the most powerful safety nets is simply getting people to engage in the change and take part in co-creating the future. One less obvious safety net is a forum to talk about what is going on and to create a sense of community. This can be done both at an individual and at a group level. Create ways for people to communicate with others about what is important to them.

Establishing Role Structures for the Change Effort

Figure 4.1 represents the role network, first presented in Chapter Two, for fostering change in a large organization. Each of the boxes is a role grouping, while each of the lines with arrows is an activity grouping. Planning, establishing, and operating this role structure enables Task IV. It provides structure and flexibility for the overall effort and defines work for all parts of the organization. The leaders established in Task III will now find themselves embedded in this overall set of activities and will be facilitating the processes in the diagram.

This role structure creates a sanction for the work of change and focuses responsibility in the organization as to who will do the preparatory work. As stated earlier, the existing organization contains the norms, beliefs, and behaviors that maintain the current state. The only people who can detect those and act on them are

Figure 4.1. Role Network for Change.

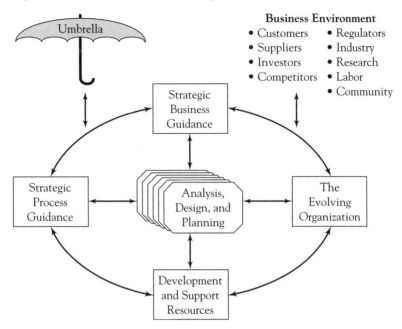

the people who live with them every day. It is up to these people to identify and modify norms, beliefs, and behaviors as necessary to facilitate change. This work is often like peeling an onion, and it takes time to work through each layer. For that reason, the processes that support the role structure are based on dialogue and are highly participative. The roles are described more fully below.

Strategic Process Guidance Team

The Strategic Process Guidance Team provides leadership for the change effort. The members of this team provide education, counseling, direction, facilitation, and support to the Strategic Business Guidance Team; the Analysis, Design, and Planning Team(s), and the Development and Support Resources. This team can include people internal or external to the organization. Its membership should include at least one person who has experience with the organization planning and development methods in the type of setting in which they will be utilized. Their collective work is to maintain consistency in the methodology and to support the strategic changes occurring within the leadership of the organization.

Strategic Business Guidance Team

The Strategic Business Guidance Team provides the guidance for change leadership. This group defines the strategies for the overall organization change effort, "sanctions" the undertaking, and provides needed resources. It usually consists of the formal organization authority for the highest level that the proposed change will affect, plus supporting resources. For example, if the change targets an entire company, the Strategic Guidance Team includes the executive team. If the change were taking place at a single site, it would probably be made up of the local leadership. In either case, the team might also contain other critical people, such as business advisors. It should have representation from the Strategic Process Guidance Team, as the overall process should be viewed as a strategic effort. One of the most commonly identified failures in large-scale change is for the ultimate authority for the change to delegate responsibility for it. Although it may seem to show a tremendous commitment for a CEO to assign a key executive completely to an effort, a more powerful statement of commitment is for that CEO to commit herself or himself to the effort (Nadler, 1998).

This team establishes a structure in which key individuals come together to take responsibility for the organization's future. It is not a "steering team," but supports the Analysis, Design, and Planning Team(s), as needed, for accomplishing the organization analysis, design, and implementation planning. This team identifies people for the Umbrella Group and manages relationships with them. It also defines and manages the process for the selection of the Analysis, Design, and Planning Team(s). Another key piece of work is to "charter" the Analysis, Design, and Planning Team(s) and provide them with boundaries, business strategy, and process guidelines.

The Umbrella Group

The people in the Umbrella Group are identified, recruited, and "cultivated" by the Strategic Business Guidance Team. They will probably never actually come together as a "group" and may not even know one another. The members of the Umbrella Group are to be a weather vane for the Strategic Guidance Team and the Analysis, Design, and Planning Team(s) in the organization planning and development effort. They provide a buffer for the organization planning and development effort with the various stakeholders. They must stay close enough to the process to provide their constituencies with needed assurances and head off unwarranted or premature reactions.

In Task III, you looked for leadership throughout the organization. Now, you look for places where pressures are exerted and where the organization can be significantly impacted by the actions of a few. Your intention is to build a system of allies who will work with you to shield the organization and the change effort from potentially disruptive events and to create conditions that will allow freedom to change or at least will serve as listening posts to provide early warning for events.

At a minimum, the Umbrella Group should consist of the executives or managers and sponsors who hold responsibility for overall financial performance of the organization. Members may come from closely associated groups. Take, for instance, a business unit moving into e-commerce. The change effort would require close associations with information technology and financial processing groups. Decisions made inside the business unit would have significant implications for both those groups. Also, decisions being made in both of those areas could significantly impact the business unit's ability to proceed.

The members of the Umbrella Group have to be kept in close contact with the change effort as it evolves. Members must hold both the interests of the change effort and of their own work areas in mind while making decisions. This role is not one of review and approval, but one of working to create the forces and conditions at a broad level to facilitate the change effort.

Analysis, Design, and Planning Team(s)

The Analysis, Design, and Planning Team(s) orchestrates and provides leadership to the work system planning and development processes, ensuring that the work system design and transition plan are responsive, accurate, and progressive, and that members of the enterprise and the external stakeholders are committed to it. This group will contain representative membership from both the Strategic Business Guidance Team and the Strategic Process Guidance Team, as well as interface with the Development and Support Resources and the Evolving Organization. Typical membership would be a mixture of people from the organization who collectively hold broad knowledge of the overall organization, its culture, its strengths, and its limits. Their primary work will be supporting the organization change planning efforts. This requires them to learn the process and to commit their time and energy to supporting it. Although they may also be experts in the business, their job here is to use their expertise to ensure that the process is engaging the right people at appropriate times, rather than to design the future state. Operating in this role requires the following:

- Learning

- Personal involvement and commitment

- Communication skills

- Knowledge of how to plan and facilitate workforce involvement

- Leadership

- The ability to make critical decisions

The Analysis, Design, and Planning Team(s) learns work system analysis and design and implementation methodologies and then leads the work force in planning the changes. It is important to note again here that the team's key role is in *planning* the structures, events, and processes that ensure that the organization is doing the work of change, rather than in doing the work.

During the course of change in a large and complex organization, multiple integrated teams may be required. Ad hoc teams may be used around specific tasks or cross-organizational issues. However, even if a team only comes together for a few days, part of the members' responsibility during the integration effort is to ensure that their approach is consistent and that they obtain strategic input from the Strategic Guidance Teams.

Development and Support Resources

Development and Support Resources learn work system analysis, design, and implementation methodologies and help the Analysis, Design, and Planning Team(s) guide the organization's work force as needed. Later, they will become training and learning facilitation resources for the development of competencies, work processes, and team processes within the evolving organization's work units or ad hoc task teams. Development and Support Resources may come from different places, but they must coordinate their work as a unit.

The Evolving Organization

This is the most important role structure for the ultimate change process: The people whose work and work lives will be impacted by the change. The members of the organization have their own approach to change. They come in roughly three varieties: Early adopters (about 15 percent), habitual resistors (about 15 percent), and wait-and-see mainstream (the remaining 70 percent)(Rogers, 1995). This mainstream group is the major thrust for sustainable change. Many change efforts spend a great deal of effort on the habitual resistors, holding them up as examples of how important it is to have a good rollout and good methods to manage the resistance. Although history teaches us that a very small resistance movement can have a powerful impact in a large organization, it also teaches us that the majority of people act responsibly and maintain structures necessary for stability and growth. It is this responsible majority who become the focus for the evolving organization. These people work hard to maintain the current state because that is the responsible thing to do. Task IV, using the role structure and processes, creates the conditions for the members to be able to do the following:

- Picture themselves in the vision

- Participate in the change implementation planning

- Understand the what, when, why, and how of the process

- Identify their "piece" of the change and carry it out in their work

- Communicate successes and failures to change leadership to ensure learning and effective deployment of the change throughout the business

This process effectively validates the change effort as real work with a positive end state. Getting a large segment of the organization into the work of change creates an incredible pull toward the future state and begins enabling change in ways that would never have been imagined by a small planning team. All of the role structure is intended to provide information, direction, and resource to the people immediately involved in the next tasks of the change. The subsequent ongoing engagement ensures the strategic alignment of Task II. Use Exhibit 4.1 to think through your role network.

Establishing Widespread Understanding of the Change

The major difference between an imposed change and a participative change is the timing of the workforce involvement. Every

Exhibit 4.1. Role Network Planning.

Proposed Change:		Primary Responsibility:	
		Support:	

Proposed Member	Roles	When Involved	Support Required	Engagement Plan
Strategic Process Guidance Team				
Strategic Business Guidance Team				
Umbrella Group				
Analysis, Design, and Planning Teams				
Development and Support Resources				
Evolving Organization				

organization change has some element of forced change. The role of change leadership is to help frame how much of the change is truly open to the creative process and then to create the conditions whereby the broadest segment of the organization can work to create the future state. This process starts by widely communicating the state of the system, the case for change, a compelling vision for the future, and the change strategy to the work force. This creates a base from which people can engage in creative learning. Although it is helpful as a support mechanism, posting the business case on the web or laminating it onto pocket cards is not adequate. The information must be put forth in a way that people can see it and engage it.

The goal is to educate the organization about the emerging possibilities and the leadership's vision for the future. People cannot develop energy for problem solving if the problems are already solved. They have to have a clear sense that the vision is set, that there are compelling possibilities for all of the organization, and that there is a space for everyone to work to get there. In moving a large organization, it is critical that the people all be working toward the same vision of the future.

As stated earlier, every engagement is an implementation step. This engagement network, the first major implementation event, comes *before* the major changes have been decided. Creating widespread understanding of the business case for change does two things: first, it sets the stage for the events and process to come and, second, it begins to engage the thinking of the larger workplace.

Developing a Dialogue About the Need for and the Selected Approach to Change

A dialogue at this point focuses on the larger organization's understanding of the desired future state, but also on the broad picture of the current state. As this dialogue unfolds, both the organization and the change leadership will begin to understand both the benefits and the costs of the change better. This is usually best accomplished in large-group sessions with a singular focus on the change itself. These sessions generate huge amounts of data relative to the change, which is then consolidated and fed back to all parts of the organization. This is, again, intended to paint as broad and accurate a picture of the proposed changes as possible.

This dialogue process is, in itself, another significant intervention. Every person who participates will, at least in a subtle way, begin changing as a result. It is not unusual to see significant energy created in the organization—with some parts even moving to action. However, this can be too much of a good thing. You are not ready yet to define the change at an actionable level, so there is a risk of losing strategic alignment by moving prematurely. The energy at this point must be funneled into the work required to create the change processes for the larger organization.

Beginning Appropriate Education Processes for the Entire Organization

Sustainability relies largely on an informed membership in the organization. A different future requires that the people know and think about different things than they do currently. This is the time for both specific and general information. It is important to create a stream of information relevant to the future state that can be used both to release the hold of the current state and to allow informed action toward the future state.

People's knowledge of the strategic business direction is of primary importance. At a more pragmatic level, organization members may not always know the actual terminology or business pressures that shape the business case for the future. It is often like receiving a message that is largely in another language. Many examples exist of organizational leadership that has very clearly shared the business case and goals with the organization only to find that the message was lost because a majority of the people did not understand its meaning and implications. It is very important to ensure that relevant business practices and subsequent reporting mechanisms are widely known throughout the organization. Now is the time to establish processes to enhance business literacy in the general work force and to share business information.

For example, consider a manufacturing and distribution facility in a company that is beginning a change effort to manage a technology enabled supply chain. The people at the work site are asked to redesign their work practices to optimize their own capability to receive orders and then to manufacture, package, and ship the product. In order to begin the process of design, employees must learn about the technology used in the system, the objectives of the supply chain, and the financial aspects of inventory and control. After they have this education, they will be able to produce an effective design.

Creating and Supporting Ongoing Dialogue

Our worst vision of hell is created on a blank screen. Longstanding management practices have supported keeping things quiet until all the answers are clear. This practice is often implemented with the best intention to prevent anxiety in the workforce and to minimize the negative impacts of change. Our experiences, however, indicate that this practice actually increases the tension in an organization faced with change. People usually know that something is happening. However, the less they know, the more they worry. The Ten Tasks are built on participation and the belief that it is ultimately the responsibility of the individual to manage his or her anxieties. However, it is the organization's responsibility to provide a forum and to validate the concerns of the members.

This dialogue process keeps the people who are less involved in the change up-to-date. The first sessions may consist of individuals venting their concerns and may even feel unproductive to those who want clear answers. Staying with the process will allow people to express their concerns properly and to understand fully where the change process is going and what the next steps are.

Using Feedback Systems

The leadership network will be a highly visible group as the change effort proceeds. They will be working to change themselves as they work to facilitate change in the larger system. A system through which they can receive targeted feedback is often beneficial to support this effort. Multi-rater or 360-degree feedback systems work well as a mirror to view their actions and effectiveness.

The intention is to provide a meaningful reflection of the ongoing organization. Because the current-state behaviors are so ingrained, some people may be unaware of how they act. Feedback relative to the impact of their behavior on others and on the change process is critical for them to begin moving toward a new set of behaviors.

Creating a More Detailed Action Plan

As the role structure is set, much more work becomes clear. Also, the processes and engagement strategies necessary for the change now have to be planned and managed. The enabling processes for the role structure must be translated into action. More complex organizations require far more detail as to how these processes will occur than do simple organizations. The Analysis, Design, and Planning Team's first work is to flesh out the action plan.

For example, in Task II you developed a high-level action plan that probably addresses your general needs for communication among different parts of the organization, general types of content that must flow across the organization, and mechanisms by which it would happen. By now, you can be much more specific about what communication has to take place, about what, between whom, through what media, when, and whose role it is to support and assure that it happens.

As another example, you know that process analysis must take place. In Task II you probably identified when in the overall process this would happen and generally how it would be accomplished. By now you should be able to define more clearly a schedule for the work, over what dates it will take place, how and where, and who will be responsible for acquiring the needed resources, coordinating the preparations, and providing guidance to the work.

As a final example, in Task II you probably identified a decision-review process for the change effort. By now, you will develop more specific decision criteria, define review responsibilities, and schedule review processes.

One of the early pitfalls in the change process can come out of the action planning. Once the processes are planned, teams are created, and the people are ready to go, the energy of the Analysis, Design, and Planning Team members may go toward ownership of the change and change activities at an inappropriate level. The key is that they reflect the organization's work and the organization's responsibility.

Summary

In many cases, the energy spent on communicating the current state and the reasons to change may seem to be a waste of time and resources. Project teams often ask, "Can't we just announce the changes to be made and get on with implementation?" From the organization's perspective, this is a largely ineffective approach.

The approach outlined in Task IV does not immediately cement change in the organization. It cements the change processes and the ability to self-regulate as the future state becomes clearer. This process appears more like an unfolding than an unrolling. This process web begins to bring together the thoughts, issues, and expectations of large numbers of people. Engaging in this thinking about the broader system level leads to the next step of analyzing processes.

Points to Remember

Everyone Has Something to Gain and Something to Lose in the Change. Change, by its very nature, has a number of unintended consequences, some good, some bad. Very often the possibility of a very negative consequence can drown out all the desirable elements of change. Use this step to help lessen the impact of the undesirables.

Everyone Plays a Role. Although we create roles in the change and designate some people to work in the change, remember that *everyone* in the organization plays some part in the overall effort and that everyone is ultimately a target of the change.

The Majority of People in Organizations Are Responsibly Maintaining the Current State. It is easy to see people who are not rushing headlong into a change as resisters and obstacles to the process. Our experience is that most people are responsibly doing what they know must be done to meet the needs of today, and until they are sure that those needs will be met another way, they will continue with what they know works. This step gives those people an opportunity to begin thinking through how this change will ultimately be handled.

Focus on the Dialogue Between the Roles of Change. Use this network to map the roles of change, not necessarily work groups. Remember that people may sit in multiple roles and will need to be involved in dialogue concerning many elements of the change.

Common Trip Points

Turning Up the Heat. Driving dissatisfaction or turning up the heat on the organization is not only unnecessary for the change, but it is often destructive to the overall strategic intent. Continue to encourage dialogue toward positive intentions and focus on what you are trying to create.

Focusing on Communicating Rather Than on Dialogue. Turning a role network into a message distribution network will only serve to slow down the change and can even turn its supporters away. Stay focused on the dialogue around enabling the change.

5

Task V: Analyzing Processes

Task V deepens the understanding of your system's processes that is necessary for good design in Task VI. Much useful documentation of process flows and requirements will be generated. However, the most important outcome of Task V is having a critical mass of people (the process analyzers) who have developed sufficient common understanding of how the organization works and must work in the future to collaborate successfully during the creative job of designing the future in Task VI. In other words, the people who will be designing in Task VI must develop an intimate understanding of the system through doing the analysis during Task V. If for any reason this will not be the case, carefully think through how you will develop the critical common understanding among the people you plan to include in the design work.

The Work of Task V

The work of Task V is to get very clear about what processes in the existing organization have to change. Task V has three major pieces of work:

- Clarifying the work system's purpose and boundaries

- Conducting a technical systems analysis

- Conducting a human systems analysis

Tasks V and VI should be approached together, as what is learned during Task V is critical to the work of Task VI. It may require special technical expertise to fully comprehend some issues, but as a rule of thumb those doing the analysis should be the designers eventually.

The depth of analysis in Task V will vary according to the depth of change you are experiencing. This chapter outlines the work required to do a comprehensive process analysis. You will have to use your own judgment as to the depth of analysis required. This may be slight, as in the case of change efforts directed toward continuous improvement, or very large, as in the case of process reengineering.

Clarifying the Work System's Purpose and Boundaries

Systems thinking has found its way into the work of organization effectiveness analysis, design, change, and improvement. On the up side, it has helped people understand what's going on with their work and their organizations and helped them to do the right things. On the down side it has opened the floodgates of jargon and analytical overkill. The concepts and labels pulled from system thinking, however, can provide a very useful framework so people cooperating in organization change can talk from the same page.

There are three basic concepts in systems thinking: process, system, and work system. These set the stage for our work in this chapter. Following is a brief description of each:

A *process* is simply a transformation, or conversion, of something into something else. For example, a process transforms inputs into outputs. The process can be relatively small or large. Transforming invoices into payments is as much a process as is transforming clinical research into a commercially available vaccine.

A *system* is an interconnected network of processes that collectively serves a purpose. Because everything in the universe is connected in some way to everything else, calling some discrete set of interconnections a "system" simply gives us the ability to make sense out of something smaller than the universe. What's important is to agree with other people about what's inside (system) and what's outside (environment). A system is best defined by its *purpose* (what it accomplishes) and *boundaries* (what's inside that has to operate well and what's outside that the "inside" has to deal with). For example, my house has a heating system with a number of interacting processes. The thermostat sends signals to the furnace. The furnace then transforms air into warmer air. A blower transforms stationary warm air into wind. Ducts transform air at the furnace into air in the rooms, and so forth. Whether the windows and doors are open or closed also affects the heat in the rooms, as do many other variables that could be considered to be part of the "heating system." If the big earthquake hits and our normal electric and gas supplies are disrupted and our furnace is damaged, it might be useful for us to broaden the boundaries of our definition and look at a different mix of things. But for now, the definition of purpose and boundaries of our "heating system" works for us.

A business organization is a *work system*. It transforms one thing into something else that some part of the environment values and for which the environment will give the business something of value. For example, a company can be viewed as a work system that transforms consumers with needs into loyal repeat customers. The customers like what they get, so they give the system money. Investors like this steady flow of earnings. Suppliers like having a dependable place to sell their wares, and so on. A company can therefore be looked at as a bounded system; what goes on inside its boundaries can be looked at as networks of processes. So we can come together using some pretty straightforward, common system language and modeling tools to understand a company. We can speak a common language about what we are finding and collaborate in figuring out what to do about it.

The only difference between a company and my heating system is that my heating system is under one master control, but a good part of a company is made up of human beings who are each thinking, goal-oriented, creative systems in their own right. Of course, this is a pretty big difference. A CEO can't just change the thermostat and have the rest of the system components fall into line. Adjustments to human systems take a lot more effort than that. However, how we approach understanding a human system can be just as orderly and rigorous as our approach to understanding a mechanical system.

Like other systems, a work system is best defined by its purpose and boundaries. The purpose of a work system is normally referred to as its "mission." Reaching a common understanding and agreement about the mission of a work system is a central issue. A mission statement is a statement of what the work system "brings about." This is more than simply publishing what you intend the company's mission to be—it is using that statement to define change.

A Systems View of a Work System's Mission

There are many ways to think about the mission of an enterprise, and there are many ways to state it. Some mission statements may be very inspirational statements of purpose; some may be more of a "slogan" that people print on a card and carry around in their wallets. For our work in this chapter, we'll use a work systems definition of the mission.

We have created a "formula" for a statement of a mission for the purposes of systems analysis and design. The brew concocted from this formula may not inspire people to great commitment, but it will ensure that everyone *understands the organization's purpose.* The working formula shown below generates a nitty-gritty mission statement that may give you important insights into the values that you hold and the work you need to be doing with excellence, as well as the boundaries within which you have control. A working mission statement should include the following:

- An action concept (word or phrase, such as "provides," "creates," or "completes")

- A customer concept (word or phrase, such as "for retailers")

- A product (or outcome) concept (word or phrase, such as "increased sales")

- One or more quality, quantity, and/or cost modifier(s) for the product ("significantly," "most reliable," "low cost," and so forth)

- A further defining, more specific "through" phrase that provides more detail about how the broader mission will be achieved

An example of a mission statement using this formula might be: "We provide (action) retailers (customer) with a better (quality modifier) opportunity to achieve significant (quantity modifier) sales increases (product) consistently (quality modifier) through supplying expert guidance in merchandizing that focuses customers on the highest margin products (through phrase)." This statement may not inspire saints and martyrs to the cause, but it will help to develop a common understanding of what the organization does well and what specific opportunities it has in its change.

Start by Looking Outside

To further develop our working mission statement, we must start from the outside and develop a richer appreciation of the stakeholders and the requirements they place on our working system. The questions in Exhibit 5.1 will help you analyze your stakeholders.

Such a stakeholder analysis will give further definition to the purpose of the work system and will serve to focus the analysis work to come.

Look Inside the Work System

We've set a systems definition of your work system's mission and begun to explore the mission by looking outside the business

Exhibit 5.1. Stakeholder Analysis.

1. What person or group has a "stake" in your work system and what does each want as a benefit for participation? For this analysis, the "who" may be an individual or organizational unit or it may be another process area of the new business model. Stakeholders are normally one of the following:
   - The receiver of an output or product of a process, a customer.
   - The supplier of an input to a process.
   - A regulator of what is produced or of the nature of how it is produced, such as the EPA, the Board of Health, etc.
   - An investor in the financial outcomes of a business process. In most organizational analyses, senior management and their business requirements represent the "investors" in the business.
   - The people involved in the work of a process and the organizations that encompass that work are also stakeholders in the process.

2. What do stakeholders expect from this work system (what are their wants and demands)?
   - Explore what drives the stakeholders to want what they want.
   - Validate that those expectations add value in the future you envision for your work system.

3. What are all of the actual outputs (or products) your process area will deliver to the stakeholders?
   - Of all the outputs, which are the "core outputs," the major products the process area is responsible for delivering?
   - Identify the "key customers" of the process area, the stakeholders who receive the core outputs.
   - What are the important specifications of the core outputs? How would a satisfied key customer describe the features of your core outputs?
   - If you cannot answer these questions to your satisfaction, plan some ways to gather the missing information. Face-to-face dialogues with key customers may be required here.

4. What are the inputs your process area will receive from the stakeholders?

Exhibit 5.1. Stakeholder Analysis, Cont'd.

- What are the important specifications for the inputs?
- If you cannot answer these questions to your satisfaction, plan some ways to gather the missing information. Face-to-face dialogues with key stakeholders may be required here.

5. Review the input and output derived from questions 3 and 4.
   - Which are the core inputs, those that will be transformed into each of your work system's core outputs?
   - What are the unique transformation flows or core process threads (core input-process-core output) that are represented by these input/output pairings? A unique major process thread may simply transform one input into a single core output (for example, transforming a load of dirty laundry into a load of clean laundry). Or it may combine a set of inputs into a single core output (for example, transforming products in the grocery store into a holiday meal). Or it may transform a single input into a set of core outputs (for example, a refinery transforms crude oil into gasoline, aviation fuel, diesel bunker fuel, fuel oil, and petrochemical feed stock). Or it may transform a common set of inputs into a common set of core outputs (transforming thread, cloth, zippers, buttons, and markings into a variety of sizes and cuts of jeans).

6. For each of the core process threads you have just identified, ask the following questions:
   - What is the nature of the input transaction? How is it going? What are the input suppliers saying about it?
   - What is the nature or the process thread in operation? How is it going? What are the stakeholders saying about it?
   - What is the nature of the output transaction? How is it going? What are the customers saying about it?

environment. We have a sense of how well we are doing and a stronger sense of what our *core* business is. Next, we look inside, where there are really two separate but highly interdependent systems: the *technical system* and the *human system*. Begin by looking at the technical system.

Conducting Technical System Analysis

Begin your analysis by looking at work system boundaries in light of your previous assessment of core inputs and outputs. You will need to put aside old conceptions of the organization and think about it from a fresh perspective. You may find that current roles, responsibility boundaries, and reporting relationships do not support the desired end goal. The objective of this step is to develop a common understanding of what it takes to transform the input into the products of the work system, to help people wrap their minds around the whole process. This common understanding will help you make better role structure and process design decisions later. During technical system analysis, you will focus on understanding what efforts, resources, knowledge, and information it will take to achieve and manage the core process of your work system effectively. This is different from focusing on improving the efficiency of work processes. In a technical system analysis, you develop an overall picture of what happens as inputs are changed to what you ultimately produce. You will look at what is needed to keep the system "under control" during this transformation, who is involved, what decisions have to be made, and what skills and knowledge are required. You will look at what could go wrong during the transformation process and what it would take to get it back in control.

Although you want to suspend design thinking for this task, you will also be looking for opportunities to accomplish your responsibilities during the transformation more efficiently and effectively. You will be looking for the best ways to assure that jobs are done well and that people stay on top of the things that can happen, capitalize on opportunities, and adapt to the demands of a changing environment. Exhibit 5.2 lists steps for conducting an analysis of the core process threads you identified earlier. Exhibit 5.3 provides a worksheet for you to record the results of your analysis.

Conducting a Human Systems Analysis

The *human system* is the network of human roles, relationships, and interactions that manage the technical system and the business of the enterprise. The *human system* is what most people are thinking of when they talk about "the organization." In developing an understanding of human systems, focus on the responses to two questions. The first is: "How well does today's network of human roles, relationships, and interactions manage the technical systems processes and the transactions with the environment analyzed in the prior steps?" The second is: "What characteristics of your organization and your organizational life do you want to keep as you move on into the future, and what baggage do you want to be sure you don't lug along?"

"Analysts" who have not been living in the changing work world cannot answer either of these questions. Neither can be answered for the population as a whole. You must engage the people who are doing the work today. The engagement processes of *human system analysis* provide you with two opportunities. The first is getting the real information to base your design on. The second is that you can have an impact on how people view the change. Earlier in this book, we said that the *implementation of change begins with the first encounter*. What you ask, how you conduct your engagements, and what you do with the answers will affect beliefs and expectations about the changes and about the people guiding them. Use the opportunity wisely.

Let's now take a closer look at the two questions:

Exhibit 5.2. Core Process Thread Analysis.

In your earlier work on a mission statement, you came up with one or more "core process threads" that represented the organization's most significant work. For each of the threads, take the following steps:

1. Reach consensus on a clear definition of the boundaries of the process that you are going to examine. Identify the boundaries of the process in terms of its specific output or products and where they go (the customer) and the specific input that is transformed into that output and where it comes from (the supplier). Define the specifications of the input and output using stakeholder expectations of the process you are analyzing.

2. Identify the major milestones in the process of the process. A major milestone is a natural, significant, interim change in the characteristics of the throughput as it is being transformed into the output. A major milestone is defined by the specifications for this interim product at that major milestone. Some of these specifications may come from stakeholder expectations.

3. Identify the "process variables" for each stage in the transformation. These are the characteristics of the throughput that have to be in control and the major creative decisions that have to be made. Define the control limits of the process variables. Some of these control limits may come from stakeholder expectations.

4. Look at the impact of out-of-control process variables on the process and the final product. Identify priority process variables, those that have the most significant effect on the process' ability to meet stakeholder expectations.

5. Identify "controllable actions" (collections of activities involved in keeping process variables within control limits or returning out-of-control variables to within control limits) for the priority process variables.

6. Identify the "priority controllable actions," the few critical controllable actions that have the most significant direct impact

Exhibit 5.2. Core Process Thread Analysis, Cont'd.

---

on keeping priority process variables within control limits or returning out-of-control priority process variables to within control limits.

7. Identify who is involved today and the knowledge, skills, and information required to accomplish each controllable action.

8. Construct a high-level activity flow chart for the major milestone stages in the core process thread you have been analyzing. Use this activity to highlight the assumptions you have been making about the design of the process. Challenge the assumptions and apply some creative thinking that might significantly improve the process.

9. Identify areas where some significant process design issues remain to be resolved.

10. Validate your analysis and understanding with people actually involved in today's work. (This can be an ongoing dialogue rather than just a checkpoint.)

11. Discuss your analysis and understanding with major stakeholders. (This can be an ongoing dialogue rather than just a checkpoint.)

12. Think about the information developed during the process analysis and define any themes that have emerged related to the work system's ability to meet its mission, its vision, and the requirements of its major stakeholders.
    • What are the "themes" you see?
    • What opportunities or cautions do they suggest?

13. Save any design ideas that have emerged during the process analysis.

First, "How well does today's network of human roles, relationships, and interactions manage the technical systems processes and the transactions with the environment that we just defined?"

Exhibit 5.3. Worksheet for Analyzing Process Threads.

Work System:		Primary Responsibility:	
Process Thread:		Support:	

Major Milestones	Process Variables	Priority Process Variables	Controllable Actions	Priority Controllable Actions	Who Is Involved?	Skills, Knowledge, Information Required

This question is aimed at understanding the enhancing or detracting aspects of organizational structures and processes relative to controlling the technical processes, dealing with the environment, and adapting to the future. If you have been using large-group processes with good organizational representation for your technical system analysis, you will already have a cross-section of the population attuned to the needs of the key business processes. If you have not been using large-group processes or don't have a good cross-section, you will have to do some interviewing. We don't recommend survey instruments here because, without follow-up, you can never really know what the responses are telling you. You have to get out and talk to the people doing the work to genuinely understand how the system is or is not working.

In your technical systems analysis, you identified who was presently involved in accomplishing the *priority controllable actions* to manage the *priority process variables* for your *core process threads*. These are the targets for your interviews. Basically, you will be asking them, "Whom do you talk to about what?" There are seven essential functions for a healthy organization that you will want to gather information about. We've used the acronym QUALITY to help you remember the seven items (see Exhibit 5.4).

With the data you gather, you will begin to understand the features in your present organizational structure that enhance or are roadblocks to high performance. What you will be looking for are the "social distances," facilitative pathways, and convolutions in the communications patterns it takes to get the job done. You may be having a little trouble with this advice to limit your data collection to the roles identified in analyzing only *priority controllable actions*. Many analysts will worry that this information won't be sufficient to prepare a complete design. However, you will get more than enough understanding to define the *minimum critical specifications* for your new work system. Completing the details will be the job of the people who fill the actual work roles in the new system. Now for the next question:

Exhibit 5.4. QUALITY.

Q   The function of accomplishing the core transformation process in accordance with the Qualities required by the key stakeholders (a more immediate focus).

U   Upgrading the *technical system* process in order to sustain a competitive advantage. This includes both maintenance and improvement (more future focused).

A   Adapting to variations or changes in the environment. Includes boundary transactions, adjustments in the core process, and influencing environmental change (a more immediate focus).

L   Realizing the Latent potential of the organization or its human members. Includes such activities as research, moving into new business areas, education, and development (more future focused).

I   Integrating the activities of internal individuals or work units (a more immediate focus).

T   Improving how the human system functions in order to sustain a competitive advantage (Teamwork). Includes such things as communication, coordination, and decision process improvement; reallocation of roles and responsibilities; policy setting and deployment; and so forth (more future focused).

Y   Ensuring that You (the people you are interviewing) are "plugged into" the organization in ways that enable the quality of work life required to attract and sustain your energy and commitment for accomplishing the other six functions effectively (both immediate and future focused).

"What characteristics of your organization and your organizational life do you want to keep as you move on into the future, and what baggage do you want to be sure you don't lug along?"

This question will lead to (1) an understanding of support systems requirements, how well support systems are oriented toward supporting the core processes, and what changes are required and (2) an understanding of the enhancing or detracting aspects of processes, technologies, organizational structures, organizational practices, and support systems on the quality of work life.

For this one, it can be tough separating the wheat from the chaff. The gossip about "what that jerk did to me last week" and how painful it's been trying to work with "those bozos" over in department five is fun reading and cathartic for the interviewee, but it's not what you are after here. Sometimes it is not easy to get a good handle on what to work into a design by piecing together individual interviews. Here is another great place to use large-group process. In the large group, you will not hear the brutal, personally focused data that you can in an intimate interview. You will hear *themes* and *priorities*. In the large-group setting, you can work the process to gather the data and do the critical analysis essentially in one step. The forum, process, and questions you design will be specific to the situation, but basically you will ask the people to identify and prioritize what needs to be kept, tossed, and created as they move on into the future. If it is important for understanding and design, you can follow up the large-group meeting with individual data-gathering sessions. It's a much more efficient and effective way to go.

Analyzing Major Process Threads—A Story

Because the analytical approach suggested in this chapter may be quite different from any you have used before, we provide a "teaching story" here that follows the guidelines provided above. This case will help you to understand the principles of the analysis approach; you can customize it to fit the specifics of your situation. The story is quite long. It weaves in definitions of terms that may be new to you and also includes thought processes analysts might go through. It may take you several rounds of reading to grasp the approach, but we believe it will be worth your effort. The approach gives you a good handle on the requirements of the processes without locking you into the rigid decision-making systems that are built into so many of today's process designs.

The story is about setting up a small lunch shop in an East Bay (San Francisco) suburban community. When you see an example in the story, it might be useful for you to take a few minutes to think up an example or two from the real world processes you are going to analyze.

Once Upon a Time. . . .

In our story, we've already got the location, an existing building that will need renovation to fit our process and work requirements. Because we will come up with important insights during our analysis, we have left the exterior design and interior layout and decorations of the shop open at this time.

Stakeholder Analysis

It's important to begin with a consideration of whom in our environment will have a significant influence on how we run our little restaurant, our "stakeholders." We have to know what their expectations are of us and what we will have to do to "have them on our side" in this venture. In this case, the Health Department and its requirements will affect what we serve and how we handle the food. The IRS has reporting requirements that will affect our accounting practices. The local building authority, the Fire Department, and a few other local "regulators" set expectations that we will have to deal with in design and operation. Suppliers tell us what we can and cannot purchase at acceptable costs, and that gives us a lot of information on what we can and cannot put on our menu. Of course, the bank will dictate cash flow considerations. Local competition and what they offer now and might offer in the future will also affect our choices. Additionally, there is my family with their time and financial expectations that will affect the design of jobs, cashflow considerations, and long-range investment strategies.

In short, I will eventually have to deal with a bunch of things that can't be overlooked. However, we've decided that the most important set of expectations in shaping what we do and how we do it is from our customers. Here are some of the things we know about them. Our best market opening is the "lunch bunch." They are local, not attracted from very far away. They want a pleasant place to eat; they are not a "grab a bite or take it out and rush back" crowd. They will spend only about forty-five minutes and much more will be considered an imposition. They are a little upscale in their tastes, moderately health conscious, and thrifty. About two-thirds will drive to the location and will need to park. They have options for lunch, so we will have to offer something unique to draw them in and keep them coming back. We need repeat business; the market is too thin to support a huge turnover trade.

Determine the Processes

We've churned over what we know from our stakeholder analysis, checked out our assumptions about their expectations, and decided that we will offer soup, salad, and sandwiches at the lunch hour. We want to leave the option to expand into breakfast later, but have decided not to target the dinner crowd. Next we will have to understand what it takes to run this kind of business successfully. That is, "What are the requirements of the processes we need and have to design in order to have a great place?" Well, a "process" simply turns (or "converts" or "transforms," whichever language works best for you) something (input) into something else (output). The something else (the output) for us is more than just a sandwich or salad, it's a satisfied customer who will come back and recommend us to someone else. Let's start with that definition of output (or "product" or "outcome," again whichever works best for you). We can detail and quantify those characteristics later. We could think of the input as all of the things we would pour into that effort, but let's start instead with what we might be transforming into that satisfied customer. We could define this as a potential customer who has a need for lunch food. With that need comes a set of tastes, a set of expectations about a lunch experience, a price range, a time range, and so forth. We picked up many of these details earlier in our stakeholder analysis and need to be pretty specific about them as we move ahead. With these two decisions about output and input, we have defined a *core process thread*, that is, a process we will analyze more deeply to get a good handle on the organization and operations we have to design.

Before digging in to understanding the work it will take to have the best soup, salad, and sandwich place in town, it might be worthwhile to dream a bit about what that might look like. If I sit back and close my eyes, I see a light, airy place with all the tables full. There are tablecloths, and folks are smiling and talking up a storm. Some seem to know the people who are serving them by name, and visa versa. A few people are waiting for tables, but not too many, and they are sipping on their favorite drinks and relaxing while they chat. The staff members work together smoothly, even though we all seem really rushed. I hear one customer trying to get the recipe for today's soup and another asking if there is any way he can buy some of our special house salad dressing to take home. I hear another customer wondering aloud where we found this quality of bread that she just couldn't find anywhere.

I let the dream run on a little further and then take a moment to jot down the things I saw and heard that I particularly liked. I wouldn't want to lose those good ideas, even if some don't turn out to fit in the end. In fact, it is a good idea to keep a running list of design ideas that pop up during this analysis and planning work. I know we need to suspend our "how" judgments and stay open to the possibilities as we work to really understand the needs. However, I'm just a normal human being, and I know that from time to time I will be biting my knuckles because I just had a great inspirational flash that gave me "the answer." My inclination will be to shortcut the analysis and just cut to the design. I have found that if I capture those great (and sometimes goofy) ideas when they hit, it calms the pressure so I can get on to the next analytical puzzle without distraction. I also won't lose the best ones when we get to the end of the planning stage.

Major Milestones

With that vision tucked in the back of my heart, let's get back to the nitty-gritty of the analysis work. To get a handle on the core process thread we identified, we have to break it down into a series of interim state changes (major milestones), remembering to keep focused on the *something* that is transforming (the throughput) NOT on the *tasks* we might perform to do it. We keep this focus because it allows us to be really innovative in "how" we accomplish that transformation and keeps us from being stuck in old familiar habits right now. We will put tried-and-true "best practices" in when we get to the final design. Right now, we want to concentrate on what happens to the nature of the stuff we're working with and leave the "how-to" options open. The major milestones ought to represent important and obvious state changes in the transformation of the throughput. That is a pretty loose definition, but I think we can make some good intuitive judgments about real "state changes" here. It will take some good analytical deduction on your part to locate them.

One of the decisions we will wrestle with is what size jumps to define as major milestones. If we make them too small, we're back to a flow chart of the way it works now. If we make them too big, we get no help in trying to break down the process so we can wrap our minds around it in enough detail to make good design judgments later.

Here is a first cut at defining the major milestones in the core process thread of transforming a potential customer into a satisfied customer:

- *Input*: A potential customer in search of lunch, with certain tastes, certain time and transportation available, and certain expectations about ambiance and service

- *Major Milestone 1*: A customer at my front door

- *Major Milestone 2:* A customer seated with his or her order taken

- *Major Milestone 3:* A customer with his or her meal served

- *Major Milestone 4:* A customer ready to leave

- *Output:* A satisfied customer who will come back and will recommend us to someone else

I had to make some choices to make this process segmentation, so let's review what I have done and make any further adjustments needed. First, I have to admit that I don't know a great deal about turning the *input* (a potential customer in search of lunch) into *Milestone 1* (a customer at my front door), but it is important— although I don't want to put time into thinking it through right now. With this additional thought, I'd like to change what we've written above and define that first transformation stage as a core process thread of its own and pass it to someone else to work through who will do a better job than I can. The *input* for our analytical work in this example now becomes, "A customer at my front door."

I made the next major milestone *"a customer seated with his or her order taken,"* rather than *"a customer seated"* followed by *"a customer with his or her order taken."* I did this because I want to stimulate some creative thinking about how to make that overall period more satisfying from a customer's perspective and more efficient from ours. The same is true for the next major milestone. I put the common steps of (1) the process of taking the customer's order into the kitchen, (2) the process of meal preparation, and (3) the processes of meal delivery into one major milestone. That's the way it is experienced by the customers; the interim steps are invisible to them. Again, I want to be creative about how we might address these steps as an integrated process. I've clumped the process of the customer

of the throughput we must control, that is, what characteristics of the throughput are not acceptable in terms of what we need to meet our objectives and the requirements of our important stakeholders. For example, during Stage 2 (transforming "a customer seated with his or her order taken" into "a customer with his or her meal served"), the temperature of the soup delivered to the customer can be too hot to handle or too cold to meet the customer's tastes. Fixing that could take enough time to really screw up the customer's experience or could create rework in the kitchen that cannot be tolerated during our busiest and most critical periods. We have to identify these "process variables" for each transformation stage of the *core process thread*. In the language of this analysis, process variable means what the throughput is doing. The soup can be too hot or too cold, so we have a *process variable* "soup temperature." (The term "process variable" does NOT mean the changes we might make to control its temperature, such as putting it in a microwave.) Two simple questions of use in identifying process variables are: "What can go wrong during this stage of the transformation?" and "What has to go right during this stage of the transformation?"

These two lists turn out to be just *two different ways of pointing at the same variable*. In one list the glass is half full (must go well); in one the glass is half empty (what could go wrong).

Again, remember that we are thinking in terms of what can go wrong with the throughput, for example, "temperature too hot or too cold," not what can go wrong with our process, for example, "the microwave breaks down." After you have brainstormed these lists of what can go wrong or what has to go right, convert the items into the language of process variables, descriptors of a characteristic of the throughput that has to be managed to meet our mission and not get us into trouble with our stakeholders. Again, in the example above, one brainstormed item would be "soup is too hot or too cold." The controllable action would be "temperature of the soup." Later in the analysis we will look at what it takes to keep the soup temperature within control limits (that span within which it will meet our stakeholders' expectations).

We want to get people to focus on their product and the variables that impact the quality of the product. This is a different angle on process analysis than the traditional focus on actions, roles, and responsibilities. Once we really understand the variables that drive the quality of the product, then we can talk about what we should do and *how* we should do it.

Focusing on the variables that drive the quality of the product empowers the organization to keep thinking about improving what they do and how they do it to get the product quality right. This is the framework that's required to establish the culture of continuous quality improvement.

Initially, we have gone with a brainstorming approach to get a handle on all the variables that must be kept in control during each stage of the transformation for perfect execution (as defined by the requirements of our stakeholders). However, we need to use a little common sense here. There may literally be hundreds of things we could identify as process variables. If we try to dig deeper into all of them, we might be here until Christmas of next year and get so lost in the trees that we will never see the forest. On the other hand, we must have enough detail on the most important variables to really define what our work system has to be capable of doing to meet its mission. Certain steps are required for figuring out which variables are the most important. First, cull your brainstormed list. Compare and combine items within each stage of the transformation. Do some intuitive prioritizing. Second, after you have intuitively culled your lists for all stages in the transformation (there could be a hundred or more), step back and apply the following criteria to select the *priority process variables*, the limited set you will really drill down into in the next part of the analysis. There are five criteria to apply in this selection (with credit to Jim Christensen, who coined many of the labels years ago):

1.   A controllable action can be labeled a *priority controllable action* if it is a *"Show Stopper,"* that is, if it stopped the process right

there in its tracks. For example, a burning sandwich would set off a fire alarm that would require the shutdown and evacuation of the restaurant.

2.   A *"Lone Ranger"* is something that, if out of control, gets passed on to the customer with no fixes available. In our example, that might be a time lag in any stage that pushes the whole experience outside of a customer's tolerance limits.

3.   A *"Mighty Mouse"* is something that if you catch it right when it happens, before it has time to call out "Shazam," you can handle it easily. But if it gets passed on in the process in its out-of-control state, it is very difficult or costly to correct later. For example, suppose a customer ordered vegetarian chili but the bowl is filled out of the wrong pot and the customer finds chunks of chicken in the chili when he or she is half-way through. If this error had been noticed at the filling point, it could have been corrected easily, quickly, and cheaply. If the error is passed on to the customer, we would have to disrupt operations to replace it. If the customer is a really strict vegetarian, he or she may never be back and might spread stories about the experience. All of that could be very difficult and expensive to recover from.

4.   A *"Fats Domino"* is when the dominos are toppling, something that goes out of control at one point affects a whole bunch of process variables down the line. For example, suppose a supplier is out of a critical ingredient for one of our special soups that is always on the menu on Tuesdays. That would require us to select a new soup for Tuesday. That would require us to change our regular buying and supply patterns. That would require a change to the cooking process for late Monday night. That would require a change in printing our standard Tuesday menu, and so forth.

5.   A *"Dealer's Choice"* is something that you intuitively know has a big impact for some reason other than the other four criteria that you can justify to your fellow analysts. We used to give people only the first four criteria, because almost anything important that we can think of can be covered by one or another. However, we

occasionally ran into semantic battles with analysts, so we added this catchall category. After all, it's obtaining agreement on the key variances that counts, not how you categorize them.

Controllable Actions

Now that we have a list of *priority process variables* pared down to a manageable few, we can move on to the next step, defining the *priority controllable actions* it takes to keep those *priority process variables* in control. I suggest you take a two-step approach, and remember not to get lost in the trees here either. First, brainstorm a list of activities that would be involved in controlling each variable. Let's say we have identified "appearance of the table" as a *priority process variable* during Stage 1. Activities to control this might be the following:

- Inspect tables before you seat the customers

- Clear dishes

- Remove soiled linen

- Take soiled linen to storeroom

- Bring clean linen from storeroom

- Notify people seating customers when tables are ready

- Let someone know when linen supply is low

- Reset tables

- Vacuum up crumbs

- Refill supply dishes

- Straighten up, set up

Next we combine these into "higher level" actions, such as:

- Clear table and inspect

- Change linen

- Set table

- Maintain linen inventory

Then, identify which of these have to be further explored to really understand the requirements of the work. In this case, "set table" and "maintain linen inventory" contain most of the work. So I will identify these as *priority controllable actions* to be analyzed more completely in the next step of the analysis. For each *priority controllable action*, identify the skills, knowledge, information, authorities, and special tools that are required, plus what additional work, authorities, and resources are needed to return the *priority process variables* to within control limits if things have gone wrong.

Deliberation Process Threads

Before moving on in our analysis, it is worth identifying a second type of process variable that has a different nature than the examples we have been using. So far, we've been dealing with keeping process variables within acceptable control in more linear, established, predictable transformations. There is normally a unique, predetermined outcome to this kind of process control work, and identifying skills, knowledge, information, authorities, and tools needed is enough. The other kind of controllable action, however, involves parts of a process that call for a creative decision, choice, or issue resolution before the process can move forward. Examples in our restaurant might be how many different kinds of soups to offer, what today's menu special will be, whether to accept a private party request during a holiday season, or just what a particular customer should order. These process variables are mini-processes in themselves. The inputs are knowledge and information, and the outputs are knowledge and information that did not exist before. These mini-processes are generally non-linear and non-routine, and the resolution process often "evolves" at the same time that the new knowledge and information are being created. To identify this kind of controllable action, we have labeled it a "deliberation" (Pava, 1984). It is just a last step in the process of mulling around the issues to get to the end point of choosing or deciding. The participants in a deliberation (and most involve more than one source of input) can come from a variety of locations. In our example, a choice of what soups to offer may involve what our customers might like, what suppliers are willing to deliver at what prices for what quantities, what a cook is willing to prepare on the day it might be offered, and so forth. To understand a deliberation in a *core process thread*, you might want to ask the following questions:

- What activities are involved in the deliberation?

- What information is needed and what are the sources of this information?

- What knowledge and abilities are needed?

- If this type of deliberation is presently part of the work, who is now normally involved and in what way?

- Who should be involved and who should not be?

- Who is not normally involved but should be because he or she would add value?

- What improvements are needed, if any?

Again, as with the more straightforward process control issues, there may be hundreds of deliberations involved in producing the output of the *core process thread* you are addressing. Before you start asking these questions about the deliberations you have identified, do some heavy culling and select a limited set of *priority deliberations* to drill down into. Apply the same criteria as before to pick the priority ones.

Often, people who are analyzing their work systems using this methodology feel a double bind at this point. They realize that to drill down into every controllable action would be an unmanageable task. The usefulness of going deeply into only *priority process variables* shows up in saved time, saved sanity, and saving themselves from being lost in details. On the other hand, they worry that they will miss something. When these concerns hit, it is helpful to remember that your ultimate job is *NOT* to design all the processes that accomplish all the work and solve all problems in your organization. Your job is to put in place an organization that has the right clusters of roles, responsibilities, skills, knowledge, information, tools, resources, and authorities in a way that jointly optimizes the needs of the business, the needs of the processes, and the needs of the people. It will be the people who work in that streamlined structure who will ultimately work out the details in the most effective way possible. Your first-hand knowledge, enhanced by the "education" you have gained by working through the tasks of this methodology with your colleagues, will give you more than sufficient understanding to perform your design and implementation planning job well.

About this time, it can be valuable to draw up a high-level activity flow chart for the *major milestone* stages in the *core process threads* you have been analyzing. By doing this, you will realize the assumptions you have been making about the design. You can test your assumptions and see where some additional creative thinking is required or some significant design issues remain to be resolved. It will give you the opportunity to test how well your process picture works for you and whether you are ready to move on to exploring the present organization to understand what needs to be kept, tossed, or created to make the process vision a reality.

OK, let's recap what we have done in this story, or case example, that prepares us for the tasks ahead. We have walked you through the stakeholder and core process thread analysis discussed earlier in this chapter. The outputs are (1) an appreciation of the requirements for success the environment will place on your work system; (2) the specifications for the products to meet those requirements; (3) the critical variables in your transformation process that you have to keep in control to be successful; and (4) what it takes to keep those variables in control.

While accomplishing the work of Task V, you have developed a common definition of the work system purpose and boundaries, and you understand the core processes required to enable it, the requirements for support systems, and the impact of present organizational structures, boundaries, and processes. Along with that, you have developed a better understanding of how close the current organization is to being able to deliver on these requirements and how much tolerance for change will be needed in your design work in Task V.

Summary

By this point, you will have accomplished the core work of Task V. You will have a good definition of the work system purpose and boundaries. You will understand the core processes required to enable it. You will have requirements for support systems, and you will understand the impact of present organizational structures, boundaries, and processes. Along with that, you have determined how close the current organization is to being able to deliver that and have developed a group of people who are ready to move into design.

Points to Remember

Two Interdependent but Different Systems Exist in an Organization, Technical and Human. Don't confuse them and don't ignore the interdependence and try to understand one without considering the other.

Analysis Is a Learning Task. It is meant to educate people so they can prepare a useful design and should not be viewed as an exercise in diving into minutia and filling the halls with flow charts and issue lists.

Analysis Is an Opportunity to Expand Involvement. Take a good look at the potentials for large-group processes for organization change work.

Remember That Implementation of Change Begins with the First Encounter. Even the simple act of gathering information or conducting an as-is analysis is a change intervention. Conduct yourself wisely.

Common Trip Points

Moving to Design Too Quickly. There can be a tendency to lose sight of the learning aspect of this task and prematurely move deeply into design possibilities. Stay with the process, documenting your design ideas and inspirations for use later.

Becoming Lost in Design Possibilities. There is also the danger of becoming caught up in the creativity of the moment and building more possibilities than can be explored. Balance the creative and the critical thinking during this phase.

Doing Problem Solving During Analysis. Don't lose sight of your objective to design a better world for tomorrow by getting stuck in problem solving in today's world.

Losing Touch with the Rest of the Organization. As soon as a group of people moves off into the analytical work of understanding systems, it is easy for them to forget about the rest of the organization, out there, waiting with bated breath for the results.

Narrowing the Level of Participation for Design. There is an inherent temptation to bring a few key people together to pull the design together quickly and accurately. This can be counterproductive, as it can easily undermine the commitment already built in the larger organization. If this is the case, the time saved in design is offset by the ensuing requirement to re-engage people and rebuild commitment.

6

Task VI: Designing Processes, Work, and Boundaries

Design is an intuitive act, not a logical solution to a defined need. A design emerges from a pregnant void amid a flood of information. It is an "ah-ha" experience, not a "from this we see . . ." proposition. At the end of Task V, you have a cadre of people who understand the work system and are saturated with information and possibilities. These folks are the ones who will be working on design.

The Work of Task VI

The work of Task VI progresses in a truly iterative fashion. However, for ease of presentation, we will explain the work and outcomes of the task in a linear format and discuss each element separately. This task has three major pieces of work:

- Jointly optimizing the work system requirements
- Clarifying the organization structure
- Creating a provisional design

The components of the design process are dealt with in an order of priority, but not in sequence. These small pieces of work, like the overall framework of the Ten Tasks, overlap and cascade into the next. This can be frustrating to people working through a design because it sometimes feels as if they are "spinning in place." Because you are dealing with a complex system, a change in one area always has impacts in others. The design process requires evaluating these changes as they occur.

Designing for High-Performance Joint Optimization

An enterprise needs three things to survive and prosper: *money, people,* and *customers.* Money comes from business profits and investors who believe in that profitability. Loyal customers come from the reliable delivery of quality products and services produced by its operations. Dedicated people come from the opportunity to have a high quality of work life. As we said in the opening chapter, over the long run, none of these three areas (business needs, operations needs, people needs) can be optimized at the expense of the others. For high performance, every capital investment, structural design, and operating decision has to embody a joint optimization of business opportunities, process effectiveness, and the quality of work life required to attract a motivated workforce.

High performance is what an organization *does,* not how it looks. High performance simply means consistently delivering on all of your goals, not whether you have exciting new structural or process configurations. How a high-performance organization should be configured to jointly optimize business, processes, and human requirements will depend on the situation. However, a look at organizations that meet high standards shows a tendency for them to have many characteristics in common. They all have a strong focus on the customer and their product. They are well-aligned with their environment. They are adaptable. They control the variances in their core processes at the source. They provide the opportunity for a high quality of work life for all of their members.

Many of these high-performing organizations also share some structural and process similarities (Cherns, 1976; Hanna, 1988; Nadler, Gerstein, & Shaw, 1992). Many have process-oriented organization structures, rather than the more traditional functional silos. The empowered "work team," rather than the individual jobholder, is the fundamental building block of their organizational superstructure. Their support systems and organizations (such as information technology, human resources, financial administration, training and development, purchasing, and so forth) are focused on facilitating the core process that produces the product that the customers want. You will find "response-able" people empowered to control variance at the source and adaptively deal with contingencies and the environment. You will also see management roles and processes more oriented toward strategy development and leadership than toward operations and control.

However, the "it depends" rule still prevails. Many organizations have tried to achieve high performance by mimicking the structure or process characteristics of the organizations they envy or admire. Without a fundamental understanding of their own situations and what it really takes to master their specific world, the result is often a disaster. A cry from the quality movement of the last two decades is: "Steal shamelessly!" Good advice. A caution from the high-performance work systems design work of the last five decades is: "You better know what you are doing!" One example is the "just-in-time" inventory systems developed in Japanese manufacturing plants in the 1980s to maximize rapid feedback on processes to keep them from creeping out of control (Deming, 1986). More than one American company only understood it as a way to shave expensive in-process inventories. They installed copies of the procedures without the depth of knowledge of their own core processes. What many of the American firms tragically got were "just-too-late" inventory systems when their core process did not deliver. Another example was the rush to self–managing work teams in the 1990s. Promises of being able to "reengineer" the major processes of the corporation stimulated quick-fix cost-cutting objectives at the expense of thoughtful redesign and the people side. Suddenly a spotlight was focused on the success of the team-based installations where joint optimization had been thoughtfully worked through over the previous three decades. Many teams that were installed in work systems that were not jointly optimized withered inside incompatible structures.

Exhibit 6.1 provides some guidelines for achieving joint optimization.

Technical Systems Design

In the systems analysis language we are using, the technical system represents the core value-adding transformation process that converts resources from the environment into the products that are "the reason for being" for the enterprise. The mission of the work systems is embodied in its *technical systems*, so this is the place to start the design process. The work system design should be built in the following order: Environmental requirements define product requirements; product requirements define process requirements; process requirements define functional requirements; functional requirements define organization structure and resource requirements; and the principal of joint optimization defines how the ultimate balance among all of these requirements is handled.

There are three sides to *technical systems design:* (1) the core transformation process, (2) the technology, and (3) the information and control system. The first application of joint optimization occurs in the selection and integration of these elements.

Core Transformation Process

The first side of the technical system design is the transformation process that converts inputs into outputs. One type of transformation process may follow natural laws, like those of a chemical transformation, and may not be open to too much "design" discretion. A second type of transformation process may follow a preferred sequence, such as the assembly of a car, the calculation in an algorithm, such as figuring out your taxes, where process design is

Exhibit 6.1. Guidelines for Achieving Joint Optimization.

Here are some rules of thumb for that joint optimization.

- Keep a strong focus on increasing effectiveness and flexibility in controlling processes and dealing with the environment, not just on designing structure, using teams, or implementing a flashy initiative.
- Assure that the output requirements of work units are formalized and well-understood by the people, that their impact on the end product is clear, and that the work units will have access to their customers for feedback.
- Assure the sources of variance during the transformation process are well understood.
- Control variance as close to the source as possible.
- Locate boundaries in ways that enhance sharing information, process variance control, contingency management, and learning.
- The boundaries should not cut through the main transformation process. They should be located at the completion of a process, a product, or a natural subdivision of the product so that:

   The members of a work unit can develop identity with the outcome of their work; and

   The outcomes of the process can be measured at the work-unit boundary, providing feedback for self-regulation.
- Assure that people who need resources to carry out responsibilities will have access and authority to use them.
- Assure that work unit members are able to develop control over their own activities in achieving the unit's goals.
- Assure that work-unit members have access to all of the information they require to define and plan the work to be done, solve problems, and assess performance.
- Assure that the required variety of skills and knowledge needed to perform the work, deal with the environment, solve problems, and maintain the technical and human systems are present to the maximum extent practical.

limited by physical or mathematical rules. Here, design creativity may be very limited but still open to rethinking process assumptions by people highly trained in a particular field of science, engineering, law, mathematics, computer programming, and so forth. A third type of transformation process mainly represents agreements on "how things are done around here." These are often referred to as *business processes* and are open to a great deal of creative process improvement during design. You probably began this process improvement as you worked to understand your *technical system* in Task V. However, remember that transformation process design decisions affect *human systems* design, so be aware of this interrelationship and remain flexible.

Technology

The second side of *technical system* design is the design of *technology*— the machines, equipment, software, and such—that facilitates, shapes, and controls the transformation process. Improvements in technology often require special expertise to accomplish, are often aimed at automating human tasks, and can represent high capital investments. There are usually a great number of tradeoffs to be made in technology, and often no one (the technology specialist, the process specialist, the financial specialist, the human factors specialists, the business strategy specialist, workers in the organization, and so forth) has all of the knowledge and information to make the tradeoffs and reach optimal decisions on his or her own. The design of technology often is relegated to one or two of those specialists in the name of *efficiency* when it really should be a very interactive activity to produce truly *effective* and optimal results.

Information and Control System

The third side of *technical system design* is the information and control system that makes *adjustments* to the technology to keep its transformation *in control* and able to achieve the objectives and mission of the system. Often, information and controls have to be designed into the technology; sometimes they can be added afterward. In either case, guidance for the design of information and control systems should come from your *process thread* and *variable* variance analysis in Task V. Whether you are working with a firm natural process or a "softer" business process, people (even expert specialists) tend to measure what they can, rather than measure what is required to keep the process in control and make good contingency decisions relative to the mission. Once again, the design of your *technical systems* information and control processes will have a profound effect on the *human systems* design.

Although the place to start is with the *technical system*, this does not mean that you should finish designing the processes, technology, and controls and then move on to force fitting a *human system* structure around it and "selling" the results to the *people*. This was the big mistake in the early attempts at "reengineering" organizations. As we have said, the design of your *technical systems* has a profound effect on *human systems* design. The opposite is true also. For example, an organization we worked with wanted to install a highly integrated business transaction and information processing technology. Standardization of business processes across the organization looked very attractive from the perspective of cost saving and ease of installation and operation of this piece of the *technical system*. However, their environmental analysis told them that high customer responsiveness was critical to their mission, and their *human system* analysis told them that decentralized, delegated profit accountability was the best way to achieve this responsiveness. In this case, the organization had to back off of optimum standardization in the technical systems design to accommodate the human system ability to deliver on the customer requirements.

In another example, a chemical plant wanted to install a team-based *human systems* structure aimed at running the plant as a high-performing, highly integrated system. The original *technical system* design had placed five control rooms in the plant, each located adjacent to one of the five major conversion processes in the *technical system*. It made perfect engineering sense and provided some ease of process monitoring. However, the design required five separate crews to form around each of the five control rooms, and the natural group spirit and lack of interaction of the crews significantly stood in the way of developing an integrated operation. The original *technical system* design had to be changed to allow control from one central control room in order to optimize the effectiveness of the team-based structure.

So start with your eye on the *technical system* and your ear tuned to the *human system*. As your design progresses, you will move back and forth, nailing down decisions on one side, validating them against the other side, making tradeoffs and nailing down another decision, and so on in a rhythmical dance of creative optimization.

Human Systems Design

Human systems design is not just drawing boxes for an organization chart, no matter how frequently it is handled that way. Human systems design is strategic planning of where the work of the enterprise will be done. An organization chart and the implied working relationships is in fact a strategic plan for the operations of an organization. A good strategic business plan reflects the business intentions of the enterprise and correlates them directly with the realities of its business environment. Just like a business strategy, a good organizational strategy (*human systems design*) reflects the intentions of the enterprise correlated with the realities of its operating environment. Human system design is therefore work planning from a strategic work distribution perspective. It has to provide for jointly optimized payoffs for the organization's three major stakeholder classes: Its customers and suppliers, its investors, and the people who work there.

You begin *human systems design* at the human/machine (metaphorically or literally) interface. There are five pieces of work:

1. Distribute the work required to accomplish and control the core processes of the enterprise

2. Define the structure of the human system and the work re-quired to plan, coordinate, and support it

3. Define the work needed to deal with the stakeholders in the environment, the customers first

4. Plan the work needed to keep the enterprise in strategic alignment with its business, operating, and societal environments

5. Explore the work needed for effective organizational learning, continuous improvement, and renewal

From these, a good human system design can be built *from the bot-tom up,* or more accurately, from the center out. Note that the basis for the human system design is distributing work around the core process, not distributing people around core functional leaders.

Designing Core Process Work— The Human/Machine Interface

Your organization's core process work is at the interface of the *human system* and the *technical system* of the enterprise. The human system interfaces with the technical systems in three ways. First, sometimes the people in the work system perform tasks that are sub-stitutions for *machine technology.* An example would be taking cans off an assembly line and putting them in shipping cartons, sealing the cartons, and applying a label. Another example would be peo-ple reading information from an order form and keying it into a computerized data processing system. Second, sometimes people per-form tasks that manage the technology to keep the process in con-trol. An operator watching dials and making adjustments to control temperatures is one example. A production planner looking at the sales projections and defining production goals and batch formulas for the next two weeks is another. Third, sometimes the people *are* the technology. Scientists modeling nature with mathematical for-mulas is an example. Salesmen collaborating to define market goals following the business process established by their organization is another. Field laborers planting strawberries and picking the ripened fruit is still another. Often, the human work at the *human/machine* interface is a combination of all three types of *technical system/human system* interaction, augmented by *tools,* such as computers or shovels. The criteria for decisions about these tradeoffs is always the *high-performance organization* imperative—joint optimization of the needs of the business, the needs of the processes that deliver value to the customers, and the needs of the people who will manage the business and the processes to these objectives.

Designing Support Work

A great deal of other work is required from your front-line work units beyond that directly involved with the core transformation processes: Technical support work, such as information management and materials supply; human administration support work, such as pay systems and accounting systems; and strategic and boundary management work involved in adapting your purpose, structures, and processes to present contingencies and the evolving future. In high-performance work systems, core process work absorbs support work to the extent that it enables a more efficient and cost-effective way of doing business. The absorption of support work into core process work also often opens QWL enhancement options to people performing core process work and to people stuck in support work "ghettos."

For example, many production lines have clear distinctions between the work of "operators" who run the lines and the support work of "set up" people who adjust and calibrate the machines, "mechanics" who do maintenance work on the machinery, "electricians" who do maintenance on the power systems, "electronic technicians" who maintain the instrumentation, "system technicians" who program the computer drives for process control, and "grunt workers" who clean up after the others. Each group works to its own objectives and pacing, often in ongoing conflict with the timing and pacing of the other groups. In more modern designs, the job of "keeping the lines running" (the core process) becomes everyone's joint objective, rather than only the job of the operators. To help this process along, many of the tasks performed by the support groups can be integrated into the work of the operators, providing them with more control, an opportunity to learn new skills, and an opportunity to increase variety in their jobs. It also offers the people from the different support groups the opportunity to move into the more enriched core process operations work, specialize in the more unique aspects of their craft, or become more multi-crafted doing specialty work. You can imagine the same scenario for the white-collar office.

At this time, it is worthwhile to talk a little about "support" work versus "core process" work. In the first place, the terms "core" and "support" do not indicate a difference in importance. If I am lifting a heavy stone, my muscles are involved in the "core process work" of relocating that stone. I don't think that it is less important that my heart keeps beating to "support" that movement. The main differentiation is which process is the "customer" that defines the joint requirements, and which process is the supporting supplier adapting to the needs of the customer. How fast my heart has to beat is defined by how much blood my arms need to move the stone, rather than the other way around. My supportive cardiovascular system will have its reasonable limits, which have an influence on the size and number of stones my arms are capable of moving around. Pushing blood through a lot of arteries is an absolutely critical facilitative and survival capability of my overall "work system." I sincerely appreciate my heart and thank my heart every morning for allowing me to get up and get on with another day. But pushing blood through a lot of arteries is not my primary reason for being in this world and I hope it will not become the defining principle of my existence.

However, if I look at my cardiovascular system as a "work unit," pushing blood through a lot of arteries *is* that work unit's primary reason for being. My muscles, my brain, and my organs are all its customers; fresh blood is its product; and blood circulation is this cardiovascular work unit's "core process." In accomplishing its core process it needs "support work" from the nervous system, the digestive system, the pulmonary system, and so on. So once the *support system* requirements are identified for the core processes, you can proceed with support system analysis and design using the same approach and rules of thumb you applied to core process work design.

As a rule, a high-performing organization has support systems focused on providing what the people need for managing the work system's core processes, for dealing effectively with its environment, and for accommodating their own needs. *Its support processes are designed to meet the core process requirements of their customers, rather than being oriented toward what is best for the support system.*

Quality of Work Life

Two parts of the joint optimization puzzle, meeting business requirements and meeting process requirements, are generally well understood. The third leg of the stool, meeting the quality-of-work-life requirements of the people, is sometimes not as well understood or is systematically ignored. For some managers, quality of work life means: "Pay them enough to get them in the door; give them enough creature comforts to keep them quiet; and move them around enough to keep them from getting too bored." For many people, QWL means benefit issues such as pay, medical coverage, length of the work week, and so forth—the kinds of things Fredrick Herzberg (1976) called "hygiene factors." Hygiene factors tend to keep people at a company, but they don't help their motivation for being productive.

A survey of motivational studies accomplished in the early 1960s identified six dimensions of human psychology required for sustained productive activity in organizations. The survey was done as part of efforts to develop systematic analysis and design methodology aimed at replicating high-performance work systems discovered in the coal fields of Wales in the late 1940s. It produced a way to quantify "the mystery" out of the notion of *quality of work life*. The six dimensions were first applied in action research at a refinery complex in Great Britain, then the Scandinavian countries, and subsequently in high-performance work systems designs in the United States. This definition of six core psychological requirements has stood the test of time. The requirements form reliable criteria by which to judge the impact of *quality of work life* on high performance (Emery & Emery, 1993):

- *Challenge:* The content must be reasonably demanding in terms other than sheer endurance, provide some variety (not necessarily novelty), and the person must have some control over the goals.

- *Learning:* The job must provide an opportunity to learn and go on learning and to receive feedback on performance.

- *Elbow Room:* The job must provide an area of decision making that the person can call his or her own.

- *Social Support:* The workplace must provide support, respect, and recognition for the value of what the person does and who the person is, and the demands placed on the job have to be compatible with the requirements of the person's life outside of the job.

- *Meaning:* The person must be able to relate what he or she does to the "whole product," feel that the product is valuable and worthwhile, and feel that the work itself has meaning and dignity.

- *Desirable Future:* The person must feel that doing the job leads to some sort of desirable future (not necessarily promotion).

A Well-Designed Job

We can wrap the principles of high-performance work systems, the rules of thumb for human system design at the interface with core process and support technology, and the QWL principles together and obtain a set of guidelines for a well-designed job. This is the joint optimization decision from the viewpoint of the *people who will actually be doing the work*. The list is an important scorecard for your designs because in the hustle of getting the new systems defined, the *people* often receive last, if any, real consideration. However, the *people* are the energy source to make it happen. The cleverest technical designs or organization structure plans may look great on paper, but if they don't deliver to the front line, the engine is going to run out of steam in no time at all and you will be back at the drawing board.

Checklist for a Well-Designed Job

- Uses an individual's skills and abilities

- Is reasonably demanding and presents some degree of challenge

- Provides opportunities for learning and development

- Provides a defined area of responsibility, together with the opportunity to exercise discretion and make decisions

- Provides the experience of responsibility for the outcomes of the work

- Makes an identifiable contribution to the eventual product made or service provided to the customer

- Provides the experience of "response-ability" to influence the qualities of the eventual product or service in a positive way

- Provides knowledge of the actual results of work activities

- Is thought of as worthwhile and meaningful by the person doing it

- Provides for variety in the range of tasks performed

- Provides an opportunity for positive social relations with colleagues

- Leads to some sort of desirable future

- Provides equitable compensation for knowledge and contribution

Clarifying the Organization Structure

One deep and abiding question for the design task at hand is how people will work together. There are a number of different choices for organization structure. Before making choices about structure, we must develop an understanding of the different types.

The work of Fred and Merrelyn Emery (1993) has strongly influenced our thinking and practice in the area of organization principles and structure. The Emerys' work details the impact of three design principles (DP) on the quality of work life and workgroup dynamics. They use the terms DP1, DP2, and DP3 to illustrate these concepts. DP1, redundancy of parts, illustrates the typical bureaucratic organization. DP2, redundancy of functions, illustrates a democratic system. DP3 indicates an error state, laissez-faire. These states were identified by laboratory research by Lewin and Lippitt, then later extensively researched by Lewin, Lippitt, and White (1939) in a series of studies. The Emerys' work, as is ours, is further influenced by Bion's (1961) work on group dynamics.

We have adapted this model through our work and expanded these notions as informed through our practice. We find there are three basic *genotypes* of organizational form. All others emerge or are some combination of these. Each *genotype* is more than just a variation in structural form. It embodies its own unique operating principles, organizational philosophy, and organizational paradigm of beliefs about organizations—how they should operate, the appropriate roles of the people in them, and the "right way" to do things. We have found that the differences are not simple alternatives; for many people, they represent differences in their fundamental ideologies. We've called these three basic types OP1, OP2, and OP3, standing for different operating principles, organizational philosophies, and organizational paradigms. We view each of these, or a combination of them, as a valid choice for design intent. We also present the impacts of unclear intent in a work group through mixed modes.

A little exploration of the "rules" and differences may help you avoid some major pitfalls in your design work. We have seen design teams, managers, and work groups defeat themselves again and again in their attempts to produce effective organization when they did not have an adequate grasp of the basic concepts underpinning what they were trying to achieve.

OP1: "Traditional" Organization—Bureaucratic Structure with Autocratic Decision Processes

Bureaucracy was invented decades ago to overcome the evils of feudal control over democratic townships. The idea of autocratic decision-making processes simply says, "The buck stops here," no matter how participative and collaborative an OP1 culture may be. OP1 structures have given us the industrial world and all its technology and amenities. The principles of bureaucracy were outlined and documented by Max Weber (1947). The term bureaucracy comes from a French word for dressers or *bureaus*. You know, the big drawers had smaller compartments in them, and those had smaller compartments in them and so on. The idea was "a place for everything and everything in its place," so to speak.

In OP1, the organizing principle is *role and role structure*. If you see someone doing something and wonder why, the answer is, "Because that's his or her job." You can't find your way around the system if you don't know the org chart. Sometimes referred to as "the rake" by the folks we have led through the Ten Tasks, OP1 basically looks like Figure 6.1.

Figure 6.1. The Rake Structure of OP1.

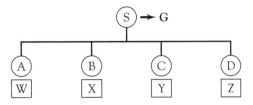

The letters in the circles in the figure represent different people with different functions. "S" stands for the supervisor. "G" stands for the goals of the work unit, and the letters in the boxes stand for the different kinds of work the different people do to contribute to the goal. The design principles for putting OP1 together are as follows:

1. The basic building block is the individual job: one person, one functional responsibility.

2. Goal definition and work coordination take place one level above where the work is accomplished.

3. Flexibility and adaptability are provided through increasing or decreasing the number of people doing the same job [Emery & Emery, 1993].

Although OP1 gave us successful institutions, it has its downside for the people who live in it, classified below by the quality of work life criteria described earlier:

- *Challenge:* Low at lower levels; higher at higher levels. Drives higher levels toward low risk taking and high control behaviors. Drives lower levels toward boredom and non-system focused activity.

- *Learning:* Focused on assigned a set of tasks or functions. Drives people toward de-skilling.

- *Elbow Room:* Low at lower levels; higher at higher levels. Drives people at the lower levels toward dependency and abdication of responsibility. This in turn requires people at higher levels to assume more of the risk and, in turn, encourages low risk-taking behaviors at the higher levels.

- *Support:* Rewards are based on presumed relative value of functions and individual performance of tasks. Drives people toward social classes, cliques, NIH (not invented here), competitive processes that inhibit information sharing, and CYA (cover your backside).

- *Meaning:* Meaning is tied to tasks more than product, reinforcing social classes. Drives people toward dissociation from the products of the work and the overall system's product.

- *Desirable Future:* The "goodies" tend to migrate to the top. Drives people toward competition for upward mobility.

These downsides have led many organizations to search for alternative ways of organizing. Usually, though, it's the supervisor ("S") who gets the blame for the problems, rather than it being the nature of the beast. In fact, the "S" role is a key to successful OP1 organization. The "S" role's fundamental cross-functional visibility, planning, control, coordinating, and problem solving are critical to the ability of the individual contributors (A, B, C, & D) to make their contributions. It is from this fact that the dependency relationships in OP1 evolve. The "S" role is also critical in mitigating the effects of OP1 on the six QWL requirements. In fact, in stable operating conditions with highly experienced contributors, the cross-functional planning and control function can become minimally important, making the mitigating function the most critical contribution of the "S" role in the successful operation of the system.

OP2: "Team-Based" Organization—Self-Organizing Structure with Democratic Decision Processes

Here the organizing principle is *product and process*. You won't know why someone is doing something unless you know the desired characteristics of the products and the activities needed to keep process in control. Org charts are of little help, and job titles are often vague, for example, "technician" or "associate." The basic design principles for OP2 follow:

1. The basic building block is the work group ("team"). Work group members are jointly responsible for producing their product and achieving their goals and have the needed range of skills, knowledge, and authority to do it.

2. Work planning, coordination, and control take place at the level where the work is accomplished.

3. Flexibility and adaptability are provided through overlapping skills and knowledge among a work group's members [Emery & Emery, 1993].

Don't be confused by the label "team." There is a difference between a team and teamwork. There can be plenty of teamwork and team feeling in OP1; the rules of play are quite different though. To use a sporting analogy, U.S. football is more an OP1 game, soccer is more OP2, and track teams more OP3 (you'll read about that next). There is plenty of teamwork in all of them, but only one functions like OP2. The structure of OP2 is illustrated by Figure 6.2, sometimes referred to as "the egg" by our clients.

Figure 6.2. The Egg Structure of OP2.

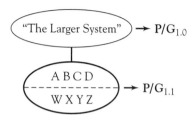

In OP2, all of the people (A, B, C, & D) are jointly accountable for accomplishing all of the work (W, X, Y, & Z) needed to meet the common goals, $P/G_{1.1}$, which is the team's "contract" with the larger system whose goals are $P/G_{1.0}$. In general, the rules for success of a work team in OP2 are as follows:

- Achieve a common understanding of the purpose and the process

- Be clear about your common values

- Allocate your resources to the most critical tasks at the moment

- Do whatever it takes, within your value system, to achieve the goals

- In your work together, keep it *together*, no surprises! If you want to stand out, be sure it's through "standing in"

- Use the flexibility you have in how you accomplish your work to "live" the principle of joint optimization

Although OP2 also has its downside for the people who live in it, its effects on the six factors for sustained productive effort in an organizational situation (QWL criteria) are quite different than those of OP1:

- *Challenge:* Set by the goal and the nature or the environment. Drives people toward cooperative goal setting and balancing challenge within the group.

- *Learning:* Stimulated by the need to do "whatever it takes" to meet the group's goal. Drives people toward "learning how to learn" and sharing knowledge.

- *Elbow Room:* Set by participative processes based on demonstrated competencies. Drives people toward appropriate responsibility level; promotes increasing maturity.

- *Support:* "We must all hang together, or we shall most assuredly all hang separately!" (Benjamin Franklin at the drafting of the U.S. Declaration of Independence). Drives people toward understanding that all the work is valuable.

- *Meaning:* Focused on the product, rather than on the task. Drives people toward association with the system's product and appreciation of the value of their work within that framework.

- *Desirable Future:* Set more by individual goals than by system parameters. Drives toward a shift from competition for promotion to more entrepreneurial, professional, or QWL notions of "career."

Because of these natural characteristics, the "S" role is less critical for OP2 than for OP1. The "boss" is really the process, and that dragon will define the work demands from moment to moment. However, living in a self-regulating democracy has a high requirement for maturity, communication, and appreciation of diversity. OP2 demands a high level of open, common understanding of the product and the process and the goals of the larger work system in which it is imbedded. In an OP2 work system, teams may be *self-managing*, but they are in no way *autonomous*. OP2 also demands an understanding of the strengths and limitations of the members of your team and a commitment to their welfare equal to your commitment to the business and technical goals. Thus, when there is a shift of organizational intention from OP1 to OP2, the transition process can take a long time to really settle in and can require very skillful leadership.

OP3: "Community"—Autonomous Structuring with Consensus Decision Processes

A community is organized around its values. The people we have worked with call this structure "the amoebae." (See Figure 6.3.)

The basic rules of OP3 design follow:

1. The basic building block of "community" is the "family unit" (individual person or work unit), each with its own goals and objectives (G_a, G_b, G_c, & G_d).

2. Community-sustaining work (W, X, Y, & Z), objective setting, and coordination take place through ad hoc teamwork, established community structures and processes, or through interpersonal processes of inclusion, affection, and control.

Figure 6.3. The Amoebae Structure of OP3.

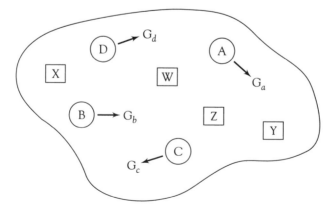

3. Flexibility and adaptability take place either through creative mechanisms of ad hoc teamwork, learning, and personal growth or are stifled through individual coping mechanisms of fight, flight, and pairing (cliques).

The easiest way to think about *community* structure in organizations is to think about the community in which you live: Separate families with their own specific goals, banded together by common values (the organizing principle for a community) about living and chipping in to provide the support systems needed to sustain the community and nurture those goals. However, people in this structure always live on the edge of disintegration of the community by the intrusion of uncommon values or corruption of the support systems. Staff groups that provide individual service to diversified customers, maintenance departments, decentralized sales forces, professional "communities of practice," the functional side of matrix organization, and so on are all candidates for effective OP3. Like OP1 and OP2, OP3 has its inherent effects on the people in it:

- *Challenge:* Generally high individual challenge. Can be too high if there is a lack of community mechanisms for getting help when it is needed. An absence of support mechanisms and positive norms can drive people toward "coping," rather than creating, and can result in feelings of personal frustration and inadequacy.

- *Learning:* Generally high individual learning requirements. Can be too high if mechanisms and community support for learning are lacking. An absence of learning support mechanisms and positive norms can drive people toward "coping," rather than adapting, and can result in feelings of personal disorientation.

- *Elbow Room:* Generally high, giving people an opportunity for freedom in achieving their own goals. If resources are scarce, who gets what resources can be

competitively set if norms supporting community cooperation and mechanisms for community decisions are
absent. An absence of these norms and mechanisms
can drive people toward coping behaviors of fight,
flight, or pairing (cliques), rather than cooperative
decision processes and creative teamwork.

- *Support:* Community action and dependence on one
another for the welfare of the whole provides an opportunity for appreciation and social support on the basis
of what one does, rather than on what one "is." If values and norms supporting diversity are absent, personal
acceptance can become a competitive issue. The absence of these values and norms can drive people toward cliques, "ethnocentric" beliefs, and prejudices.

- *Meaning:* In a healthy community setting, individuals
have an opportunity to find their own meaning in their
contribution to the community and in who they are
and what they do. If there is a marked absence of common vision and values in the community, meaning can
become overly focused on self, rather than on the
needs of the community. The absence of common vision and values can drive the community toward disintegration and the formation of splinter groups,
"ethnocentric" subcultures, and destructive competition for scarce resources.

- *Desirable Future:* Generally characterized by uncertainty about the future because of the basic individual-
ity underlying the structure of community. People must
cooperate in defining a desirable future and work together to produce the means to get there. If many of
the requirements for healthy community mentioned
above, such as common values, common vision, supportive norms, and collaborative mechanisms, are ab-

sent, there can be feelings of hopelessness and helplessness. This drives people toward fatalism, "dropping out," and dependence on "saviors," rather than on strengthening their initiative and self-reliance.

Because the individual members of OP3 pursue their own goals individually with their "clients," the common organizational work for OP3 involves the following:

- Clearly defining and reaching genuine agreement on the common values that will drive the individual practices and the community support requirements

- Establishing and maintaining effective processes for distributing access and allocation of the individual work

- Willingly diverting personal resources and "getting involved" with the community support work needed to sustain the community

- Establishing and maintaining acceptable processes for allocation of the community supporting work

- Committing to, and a high tolerance for, collaborative decision making

- Establishing and maintaining viable processes for consensus building and conflict resolution

Paradoxically, the people driven to the kind of work best accommodated by OP3 don't normally have much innate love for the kinds of things necessary to sustain it. Although the "S" role from OP1 makes absolutely no sense at all in OP3, leadership and coordination in community development, maintenance, and management is critical and sometimes requires special roles within the community. The danger is that in allocating their community maintenance responsibilities to specialized resources, they risk sliding back into OP1, losing the freedom of practice that brought them to OP3 in the first place.

Problems and Pitfalls of Designing Without a Grasp of the Three Structures

The importance of having a fundamental grasp of the three basic modes of organization can be illustrated by three classic dysfunctional "mixed modes." In today's complex world, any organization can contain a mix of the OP1, OP2, and OP3 settings. Usually the mix, if managed intelligently, can serve its purpose and provide flexibility for the business. Often, however, a mixed mode breakdown happens when the culture is one thing and the intent is something else.

The Headless Horseman

The first classic problem-riddled mixed mode represents a confusion of OP1 and OP2 that we have called "The Headless Horseman" (see Figure 6.4). It results from an intention to move to a more self-responsible team approach by merely withdrawing the influence of the "S" role without the needed changes in structure and a paradigm shift. It is a bureaucratic structure with laissez-faire leadership.

The default organizing principle, the imperative that drives how the organization actually works, will end up being the human psychology of the players, rather than the role structure, process, or values of the enterprise. The design is characterized by the following:

**Figure 6.4. The Headless Horseman
Structure of Confused OP1 and OP2.**

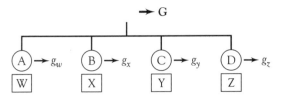

1. One person, one function, and one functional oriented goal

2. Goal definition and work coordination takes place through interpersonal processes of inclusion, affection, and control

3. Demands for flexibility and adaptability are handled through individual coping mechanisms of fight, flight, and pairing (cliques)

Without fully shifting to the principles, structures, and paradigms of OP2, the players have no basis for coming together for planning, agreement, and coordination of the overall work. People in this mixed mode can struggle along if the different functional experts already have a good knowledge of the job and the product and have a good working relationship, and if nothing major changes. However, faced with unfamiliar contingencies, disagreements about priorities, incompatible personal goals, or interpersonal conflicts, the system will break down unless one of the members steps in and takes over as the de facto supervisor. The effects of "The Headless Horseman" on the six QWL criteria follow:

- *Challenge:* Generally high demands. Drives people toward "coping," rather than creating. Often results in feelings of personal frustration and inadequacy.

- *Learning:* Generally high demands. Drives people toward "coping," rather than adapting. Often results in feelings of personal disorientation.

- *Elbow Room:* Competitively set. Drives people toward flight, flight, or pairing (cliques), rather than work.

- *Support:* Again, generally a competitive setting. Drives people toward lack of open support for the work or goals of others.

- *Meaning:* Individual, rather than system focused. Drives people toward dissociation from the overall work goal or product.

- *Desirable Future*: Characterized by uncertainty about the future and the means to get there, with feelings of hopelessness and helplessness. Drives people toward fatalism and a search for "saviors."

This particular OP1/2 situation often results in a reinforcement of OP1 and its characteristics, rather than a migration toward OP2 as intended in the first place.

The OP1/OP3 Feudal Lordship

This mixed mode results when OP1 leadership does not know how to fill the OP3 leader role. Although the players have their own practices, the leader attempts to function as a traditional supervisor, trying to "own" the goals and give work direction to individual contributors. In OP1 fashion, the leader also tries to define the values and "delegate" the community-sustaining work, enforcing those definitions through the exercise of authority. The people are placed in a "whipsaw" situation where they are, in many ways, individually accountable for the success and quality of their own work, but their decisions are often countermanded from the less informed position of the "boss." Rather than an organizing principle of commonly supported values, the organizing principle becomes one of relative *power* to enforce personal values. The design characteristics follow:

1. The basic building blocks of this mixed mode are "community," the family unit, individual person, or the work unit (A, B, C, D, & S), each with its own goals and objectives.

2. Formal goals are established, work is coordinated, and community sustaining support work (W', X', Y', & Z') is defined through authority and control of the "lord" and accomplished through member dependency characteristic of an OP1 organization. Often, however, the formal system is mitigated by informal organizations operating covertly in line with the characteristics of healthy OP3 community principles.

3. Needs for flexibility and adaptability are handled through informal organization (often rebellious "guerrilla warfare").

The outcome is illustrated in Figure 6.5.

The effects on the six quality of work life issues follow:

- *Challenge:* Generally high for A, B, C, & D; lower for S. Drives people toward coping behaviors or creating secretively. Often results in feelings of hopelessness and resignation.

- *Learning:* Generally high demands with low availability of resources for A, B, C, & D. Drives people toward "coping," rather than adapting. Often results in feelings of dependency and personal inadequacy.

- *Elbow Room:* Autocratically set. Drives people toward dependency/counter-dependency coping patterns. Often results in feelings of frustration, anger, and rebellion.

- *Support:* Generally a competitive setting. Drives people toward self-protection and a lack of open support for the needs, work, or goals of others.

- *Meaning:* Individual, rather than system focused. Drives people toward dissociation from the overall community needs.

Figure 6.5. The OP1/OP3 Feudal Lordship Structure.

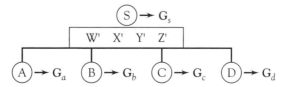

- *Desirable Future:* Characterized by uncertainty about the future and the means to get there, with feelings of hopelessness and helplessness. Drives people toward fatalism and a search for "saviors."

This OP1/3 situation often results in a reinforcement of clandestine informal organizations (often specially focused OP2s), rather than a migration toward either OP1 or OP3.

The OP2/OP3 Mindless Centipede

In this situation, a group of functional experts is brought together for some ad hoc purpose without either strong process leadership or the advantages of OP2 common process and product knowledge and commitment. The group is usually called a "committee" or a "cross-functional team." The organizing principle, rather than the *process* and the *product,* tends to be the loosely defined "purpose" of the group as modified by the personal agendas of the individual members. Often these personal agendas are spawned from commitments "back home," rather than being responsive to the higher order systems integration issue that caused the group to be formed. The structural "rules" for the mindless centipede follow:

1. The basic building blocks of this mixed mode are the individual persons or work units (A, B, C, & D), each with a different functional perspective, responsibility, and agenda.

2. "Purpose" is assigned by the larger system. Work goals G, g_w, g_x, g_y, & g_z are established by personal agenda and referent power. The work (W, X, Y, & Z) is defined and coordinated through interpersonal processes of inclusion, affection, and control.

3. Needs for flexibility and adaptability are handled through psychological coping mechanisms of fight, flight, or pairing.

The resulting picture is illustrated in Figure 6.6.

Figure 6.6. The OP2/OP3 Mindless Centipede Structure.

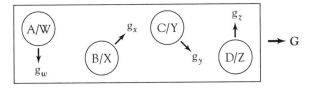

The effects this structure has on the QWL issues follow:

- *Challenge:* Generally high demands. Drives people toward "coping," rather than creating. Often results in feelings of personal frustration and blaming.

- *Learning:* Generally high demands. Drives people toward "retrenching," rather than adapting. Often results in acts of differentiation, rather than integration.

- *Elbow Room:* Competitively set. Drives people toward personal agenda oriented tactics and compromise, rather than toward creative collaboration.

- *Support:* Again, generally a competitive setting. Drives people toward lack of open support for the value, work, or goals of others.

- *Meaning:* Individual, rather than system focused. Drives people toward dissociation from the overall work goal or product.

- *Desirable Future:* Characterized by uncertainty about one's personal future and the means to get there. Drives people toward pursuing hidden agendas, political maneuvering, escapism, or a retreat to the familiar.

This OP2/3 confusion often results in a disintegration of the group or an ineffective resolution to the task. If a strong charismatic leader emerges, the configuration can migrate toward an OP1 solution for accomplishing a process and delivering a product. Or if there are sufficiently shared values about the importance of "G" (or enough fear about not getting there) and the members are relatively free from "home rule," the configuration can self-migrate to a workable, ad hoc OP2.

Selecting the Design

As explained above, there are three basic choices in how people interact within a work group: OP1—Traditional, OP2—Team-Based, or OP3—Community. Each of these structures carries with it a set of positives and negatives. When creating the change plan, designers must pick the set of conditions that most represent the desired future and then structure support systems and processes to offset the negatives associated with that structure.

Creating a Provisional Design

Because of the historic, repeating difficulties of implementing design solutions put together in isolation by small task teams, we recommend trying to move as far toward full participation approaches as the situation and the culture will permit. This increases the need to pay as much attention to fostering consensus as to accomplishing the design tasks. In fact, almost everything we have been doing in describing the Ten Tasks has been to help steer you toward developing a consensus about the needed changes. When the time arrives for *final* structural design, the issue should be the form of the *how*, not the reasons for *why* nor the scope of *what*. You should also have developed a consensus about whether you are heading for a fundamentally OP1, OP2, or OP3 solution. Although we use the term *final*, the truth is that you will be making many little design decisions along the way; what you decide here is not carved in stone.

Now is the time to put all of the elements together in a picture, with boundaries identified, functional responsibilities defined, staffing planned, and operating scenarios explained. As we said ear-lier, we strongly recommend designing from the inside out, not from the top down. However, design will probably progress in three phases:

1. Identifying the overall layout of the work system, including the design concept and the components of the structure.

2. Filling in the details for the component business and work units defined for the whole.

3. Completing the detailed design. This work is done by the people who will actually be doing the work in the work units identified.

For each phase, the objective is to define the *minimum critical specifications*, no more and no less. These are the design descriptors necessary to assure that the next phase remains true to the intent of the concept, but leaves elbowroom for the people closest to the work and the real world situation to make adjustments.

Phase One: Work System Layout

We have found it productive to accomplish the first phase in a workshop setting involving somewhere between twenty and two hundred people over a three-day to five-day period. We have worked with smaller groups and find that with fewer than twenty people the interpersonal dynamics of the group get in the way of the information dynamics for the design process. Other people have conducted successful design processes with even larger groups. If you have selected your group well, it will mirror the commonality and diversity you face with the population as a whole.

The workshop will alternate between small-group (three to ten) work and total-group work. Regardless of the procedures to accom-plish the design tasks and define the consensus, the stages of the ap-proach are pretty consistent. First, the people in the process should have worked together in some interactive way on the systems analy-sis. If the group is starting at very different levels of engagement of the situation, you will have to repeat the analytical arguments that brought you to this point. If you can't have an engaged population, you had best set a good bit of time aside to work over the core of the analysis together to get people on somewhat level ground before you ask them to be creative.

We recommend that the first piece of design work in the workshop collective should be visioning, asking the people to imagine where they want to go. In building consensus you always want to establish and expand on the common ground, not search out and hammer on the differences. The next step is to let the people do some imagination stretching on a low-risk design task and get their propensity for nitpicking out of the way. We usually accomplish this by having different small groups put together "throwaway" but realistic designs emphasizing different singular objectives. Examples of singular objectives might be: "maximize quality of work life," "maximize variance control," or "maximize customer responsiveness." We like to pick from each side of the joint optimization question, using specifics that mirror the realities of their world. We recommend keeping the objectives abstract enough that the people don't forget they are "throwaways" and get all tangled up in their own juices.

Next comes the opportunity to design for real, in small groups with mixed stakeholder interests. From this point on, the process alternates between small groups working on their design ideas and cross-group presentation and critique of what each small group comes up with. Often there is a good deal of natural convergence of ideas, especially if your designers are the same people who collaborated in the analyses of Task V and you have followed the visioning and warm-up approach described here.

Often the group is much closer to agreement on the core concepts than many imagine they might be. If there is significant diversity, you will have to exercise good facilitative skills to discover and establish the common ground among the different evolving designs, then build on this core of agreement. This can be hard work, and sometimes you can reach a place where there are two or three fundamentally different conceptual designs that are not going to yield to compromise or tradeoffs. In other words, the different approaches are just *different*, not better or worse, but based on different beliefs about how to meet the design criteria most effectively. If the group ends up with this kind of major split, refocus the group's attention on how the choice among the alternatives will be made, rather than trying to continue to drive for consensus. Often, if you have been following the principle of the Ten Tasks fairly rigorously, a group will be ready to allow management to choose from the two or three proposed alternatives. Sometimes they will allow it to go to a vote of the stakeholders. There are any number of alternative approaches to selection that the design group can agree to. The most important principle here is not to let frustration with the situation cause premature takeover of the decision process by "authority figures" in the organization. It is a move that can destroy the trust in collaboration you have built, tossing the process into a disruptive OP1/OP2 mixed mode. It can leave you in the difficult position of having to gain back the trust and initiative required for genuine collaborative implementation planning and transition management in Tasks VII and IX ahead.

The last piece of work for this conference is to list the questions remaining and the requirements for detail to be added later. The goal is to have the people in the room know what work remains to be done and who is going to do it.

Phase Two: Detailing Business and Work Units

After the dust has settled, move on to the second phase, beginning to put more detail into the design concept. Much of this requires too much work (including some analytical tradeoffs) to be completed in the workshop setting. The design returns to smaller groups who complete the specifics about what is required from each work group, requirements for support groups, and the output agreements for each work group.

After this phase, when the provisional design is fixed at the level of detail needed for *minimum critical specifications*, it must be approved by the ultimate decision makers and validated by the population.

Phase Three: Completing Design

The final phase of design is done by the people who are actually in the jobs and is completed in Task IX, Managing Transitions.

Summary

The work of Task VI has brought the requirements for the future into a provisional design of processes and structure for the organization. The work began by creating an approach to design that is consistent with the engagement strategies for the overall change. The designers, who have been immersed in the data since Task V, begin designing the processes for high performance. They begin with the technical system and jointly optimize with the human system. During the process, the group achieves the required consensus on an operating philosophy (OP1/OP2/OP3) and considers the requirements for quality of work life.

The work culminates in a provisional design that outlines the overall business and work-unit structure, the support system requirements, and the minimum critical specifications for the rest of the organization. You should remember that the design is not complete. There will be many details to finish at the work-unit level, as well as some major support systems or components of the design that have not been completed. The next task outlines the work required to move this provisional design into a sanctioned and operating plan for the organization.

Points to Remember

Continually Apply the Principles of Joint Optimization. The concept of joint optimization is central to the work of change and high-performing organizations.

Remember That All Designs Have Some Negatives. There is no perfect design. All systems are complex and carry with them a constellation of results, some good, some not so good. Pick the best set of results and establish key processes and support structures to deal with the negative effects.

Common Trip Points

Designing Incompatible Structures. The mixed modes—the Headless Horseman, the Feudal Lordship, and the Mindless Centipede—can slow down or stop your change effort as you move into the larger organization.

Overspecifying the Details. Leave the details of how people will accomplish the design intents to the people who will actually do that work. Task IX outlines the approach for engaging the change as ongoing work.

Task VII: Planning Implementation

M oving from design to implementation can be quite a shift in thinking and energy in large change efforts. People who have been hammering out the agreements of a provisional design are anxious to get on with the implementation. Senior management is ready to see the benefits from the new system. Middle managers are ready to get their departments back to normal and out of all the meetings. Everyone in the organization is looking at the new design and trying to find his or her spot in the new work system. It is typically a time of high energy, often with great anticipation of the benefits of the new system, as well as with anxiety about the impact on the individuals. It can be a real effort to pull people back into planning sessions to work out the details of implementation.

The Work of Task VII

Task VII could be described as the "invisible task." While there is nothing particularly analytical in the work, it is absolutely essential to the success of a change effort. When this task is done well, the only visible attribute will be an effective implementation. But when this step is skipped or skimmed over, its impact is seen. The design put forward in Task VI is provisional and incomplete; there is still a great deal of work remaining to enable it fully. The typical large-system design has been thought through at a very high level. It details the major aspects of the new system and the requirements of each of the major components. There will still be many questions to answer, integration points to clarify, and sections to design.

One example of this is in a business unit that used a broadly participative and highly engaged approach to move into a new business model. They began with clear stakeholder guidance and a new and creative model for the future. The process was brought through Task VI with a series of large-group events in which over one hundred people agreed to the provisional design. The effort moved rapidly to Task VII and proceeded into validation. New leadership positions were filled as the entire structure of the organization was changed, as was the focus of the various elements. The first work of the new leaders was to delegate the implementation efforts through the new management structure. The results were fairly destructive. Many new work groups were formed, and the missions of most existing groups were fundamentally changed. The work-unit designs were incomplete at this stage, and many of the support processes required to enable the new business model were not yet designed. There was much confusion and reworking over the following months. Fortunately, the people of the organization managed to settle back into business. The real negative was that the innovative features of the design were never fully realized, and within a year the organization was drifting back to its old business practices. The lesson here is to do the work of Task VII very well.

The output of Task VII is a clear plan for implementation that is grounded in the new design and takes change in the plan into consideration. A foundation of this approach to change is that *implementation is always occurring and evolving,* from the first notion of change. Each of the earlier tasks has had an implementation component, either by actually deciding the design or by providing requirements and specifications for it. In Task VII, this becomes critical. The change must be modeled in the implementation approach as much as possible. Any key assumptions must be reflected in the implementation plan. An example of this is in moving to team structures. If a team-based system is the desired outcome, the implementation approach must use teams and the implementation structure must look like the desired end state. This allows the organization to begin living out the concept immediately, even though the specifics are not yet designed.

Our Approach to Implementation

One major feature of this task is reflected in the shift of questions. Earlier tasks have defined the "why's" and "what's" of the new system. Task VII begins the strong focus on the "how's" of the provisional design, which usually has yet to be translated into actual work-unit changes. Fully engaging a change requires that all members of the organization review their work, their roles, their behaviors, and the required skills in light of the new concepts. The only people who can accurately do this are those who are doing the work (Lytle, 1998).

Another key feature of our approach to change is that design becomes the work of the organization as soon as it is practical. Part of implementation planning is to shift design completion efforts to the work groups and plan the necessary support to ensure their success. Although the workforce literally carries out implementation, the change leadership retains the important task of ensuring that the resources are committed and that the time is allotted for this work.

This can be a trip wire of working large-scale change. As change moves toward implementation, change leaders and sponsors often see it becoming more tactical and begin to focus on more "strategic" work, leaving the deployment of the design to others in the organization. Designs are commonly deployed through the formal management structure and monitored through existing processes. A common thought is that the change effort has now become easy to identify and all implementation work can be readily done by the existing or changed organization. The Ten Tasks require that change leadership think strategically throughout the implementation effort. This is especially true when the design calls for organization changes and significant shifts in the role structure of leader ship groups.

Bringing in a new leadership structure means special opportunities and challenges. If the design has significant organizational elements, enabling the new leadership structure becomes its own work—in addition to the work of carrying forward the new design.

Because the change is now moving out to an expanded group, there are many more integration issues than there have been. The broad communication network created in Task II has been working to keep the whole organization involved in the change. Because people have been involved in the change, new teams and individuals can begin working on specifics in the design more quickly. Even so, when the elements of the change begin moving out into the work units, there will still be a number of issues that have to be surfaced and resolved.

We come again to the concept of minimum critical specifications. If you attempt to design the work units without a fundamental knowledge of the overall design intent, you may end up with work groups that do not actually enable the new design concept. The way to avoid this is to use the minimum critical specifications that were so clearly defined in Task VI. These will help to maintain a common intent throughout the organization. The people at the work-unit level who complete the design will use these specifications as their guideposts.

As mentioned earlier, the Ten Tasks are not completely linear. They overlap and often require cycling back through. As a basic rule, any new group that engages the design at this point must start at Task I and work its way through. This is to allow people a grounding in the why's and what's before you ask them to answer the how's. The amount of time and effort needed depends on what has already been done and on what is required for that group. The communication network works to minimize the degree of recycling and to keep the entire organization engaged as the change evolves. Even so, there is still some degree of revisiting simply to validate what has been done and to plan from this point forward. This task has a higher requirement for going back through earlier work than some of the others.

Those doing implementation planning take the elements of the provisional design and identify what has been decided, what is left to be decided, and what elements must be changed immediately to be able to move ahead. They also determine timing for the work ahead, identify immediate work, near-term work, and long-term development work. Part of this task is also revisiting the role structures identified in Tasks III and IV and making necessary changes to the structure and processes. The work ahead is of expanding scope, so the communication network will have to be expanded to match. This task has six major parts:

- Validating the design

- Identifying further design work

- Establishing timelines for design work

- Establishing a transition management process

- Establishing integration processes and issue resolution forums

- Identifying individuals or teams to complete the work

Validating the Design

Task VI generated a provisional design for the organization. At this point, that design must be validated throughout the larger system. For a design to actually work, a critical mass of the people must agree to support it. The work of previous tasks has been to identify critical elements and requirements for the new design, so you must go back and work through a validation on several levels with a larger group of people. There is always a requirement for leadership to accept the new design. Depending on the scope of change, key stakeholders must also validate it. Timing here is the greatest consideration. In a large organization with significant changes, such as a shift to a new business model, leadership must endorse and commit to the design early. This is particularly true when the design calls for organization changes, new leadership skill sets, or changes in resource base.

This is typically an iterative process, going first to the key decision makers of the organization. This can feel like starting over to people who have already been intimately involved in the design. If the engagement work has continued through Tasks V and VI, this validation should be very simple. The more the design has been connected to the larger organization, the more people will already understand the intentions and the thought process that brought them to that point.

In this context, there will typically be some inclination on people's parts to present other alternatives and ask questions such as "Why didn't you do it another way?" This is a very natural process and should be welcomed and engaged. It is important to note that getting people's input along the way does not necessarily guarantee that they will agree with the final design. If the design has gone through significant evolutions of thought and reflects large cultural or operating changes, it may be difficult for people to see and accept. Working through the validation process should help people accept the design.

The design should be validated in light of the following elements:

- Mission, core values, and vision

- Stakeholders' wants and expectations

- Ability to control variance

- Quality-of-work-life values

Mission, Core Values, and Vision

The provisional design must have, as its fundamental building block, the ability to deliver results that are aligned with the mission, core values, and vision of the organization. Designs are typically done by smaller groups in the organization and are then brought to the larger organization. Design teams often make the mistake of presenting the details of design before people have had the opportunity to understand how that design enables the broader picture. It is easy for an individual to first look at a design to find his or her own place in it and then to begin to question details of the actual model. At this point, the emphasis should be on the overall design and its ability to accomplish the overall mission of the organization, rather than on the implications for individuals.

The key questions for the organization members are related to whether this design, in total, will accomplish the key business of the organization. It is critical to communicate that the work unit specifics are yet to be determined and that the process will allow people closest to the work to finish the details of their work processes. The spirit of this validation tells whether this design reflects the intention of the desired future and enhances the values and vision of the organization.

Another major question is who needs to accept the design. The role network map you designed in Chapter Four can be used here to help you think about who has to be involved in validation. By the time the change is all the way through the organization, every member will have performed his or her own validation. If this occurs after they have been asked to implement the change, they will often find a forum for disagreement through rejecting it or altering it. Although this may seem to be a significant delay to people who have already accepted the design, it is better to over-include at this point. At a minimum, the key decision makers and those ultimately responsible for the organization must agree to the validity of the design. The choice here is whether to have the design non-negotiable to the rest of the organization, or to have their initial acceptance be part of a larger group's validation.

Stakeholders' Wants and Expectations

Earlier work in design identified the stakeholders. Before progressing, the design has to be validated with this group. It is important to note that most of the stakeholders will simply be looking for their own critical requirements of the design. For many of these stakeholders, particularly those external to the organization, the validation does not depend on whether the design is the right one, but rather on whether their requirements have been considered and included. They expect to obtain at least as much from the new design as from the current one. This expectation can cause problems when the new design lowers the service level to stakeholders or significantly alters the existing delivery mechanism. Take, for instance, a design that emphasizes technology delivery of key information. If the stakeholder group does not value technology, their initial reaction will probably be less favorable than the design team would like. Another case may be in moving from field responsibilities to service centers. Stakeholders lose an existing relationship and possibly some customized service. This can take quite a bit of effort to work through.

In planning the stakeholder engagements, consider first the wants and expectations that were collected earlier. Ensure that the group in charge of the validation process understands these and how they were used in the work. Engage the stakeholder group in a dialogue around the impact of the changes on their wants and expectations and negotiate the best way to move forward with the design. Again, recognize that the stakeholders are a large component of the success of the overall change.

Another important piece of information is how stakeholders will stay connected in the new design. There is always the possibility during a change to have an unexpected service interruption with key stakeholders. Find out, from the stakeholders' perspective, what the worst things that might happen are and jointly agree on how these will be monitored and maintained. This will build trust and credibility and will provide focus during the work-unit design efforts.

Ability to Control Variances

The design must be able to control the key variances of the business process. This is an important element in both normal and abnormal operation. This validation is more critical than some of the others. It requires testing and generating scenarios with people who are intimately familiar with the requirements of the environment. If this is an operating system change, as in the base architecture of a financial system, then the system can be prototyped and run with test data. A group of functional experts can operate in a "sandbox" and determine to a large degree the capacity to control the process. If it is a business system change, then the change can often be tested with economic models or in a simulated environment. If it is more a relationship and hand-off change, the new system can be modeled by walkthroughs or simulations.

How this validation is accomplished is completely dependent on the nature of the change and on the environment in which it will operate. The requirement is to put the people who best know the requirements, preferably ones who have not been intimately involved in the design, into a setting that most closely approximates the intention of the design. They can then validate the capability of this design to handle variance. The output of this validation should feed the planning process for the next steps. A well-engaged provisional design rarely requires a complete recycle back to Task VI. Unexpected learnings in the validation of the process may, however, have major impacts on the completion and implementation work.

Quality-of-Work-Life Values

The quality-of-work-life values identified in Tasks V and VI now must be expanded and tested across the larger organization. Quality of work life is unique to every organization and even to the different areas within the same organization. A common error of design teams is to assume the values of others and design according to those assumptions. Many times they are right, but they sometimes miss major idiosyncrasies within the larger organization.

The design, with its assumptions of quality of work life, must be validated across the larger organization to test for fit. If the engagement work of the previous tasks has been working well, this should be fairly straightforward. Members of the organization must see their values represented in the design and agree they are supported within it.

Identifying Further Design Work

The provisional design will have many areas that still have to be worked through and resolved. It is common when significant changes in the business model are involved to have many new ways of operating within that model. For example, take the instance of a business moving into an area of e-commerce that changes the way the organization deals with the existing customer base and begins targeting a new, expanded set of customers. The new customer interface must be designed, but cannot be implemented until the overall model has been accepted and actualized. How this process changes working with existing customers and how the two processes will coexist through the transition are important, detailed design questions that will not be finished during the provisional design step.

The people who are intimately familiar with the design will document the work remaining to be done and what is still required. They will identify and list any additional design issues to be resolved, further design work to be accomplished, and implementation processes that have to be thought through and planned. Common examples for changes in a human system are the staffing strategy, process, and timetable.

Although the designers will not determine work at the unit level, they must take into consideration how the people in the units will complete the design work. The participation plan is critical here. Another common trip wire for implementation is to assume that the work units will be able to make the required changes without any support. The designers must also consider the types of support systems that may be necessary during implementation.

The last required area of planning is to clarify the *internal interface* process. Making major changes, then completing the work-unit design, creates the opportunity for process breakdowns and gaps to occur. It is critical that the work-unit designs also have plans to validate the interfaces between the work units and major processes. For example, in a change involving moving to a process-based organization, the design called for specific process hand-offs to occur between work units. Hand-offs have to be clarified in detail at each hand-off point before work-unit designs can be completed. Large-group activities are a common method for clarifying processes. It is a fairly straightforward exercise to bring people from each of the major work units together and to work through the major processes. This typically involves talking through the major processes and ensuring that each work unit's responsibilities and requirements are clear and aligned. During this time, people not only clarify their own processes, but they also learn about the entire organization's processes.

Establishing Timelines for Design Work

Identify rough timelines for resolving issues, completing the design, and planning transitions on the list. These should be detailed enough to indicate when work-unit design will start and when the design features will be completed. These timelines will provide the basis both for planning and for communications to the larger organization.

The timeline should also reflect changes that can take place immediately. There will be some key changes that enable people to live out the design in small or large ways—either by beginning new behaviors immediately or by stopping existing behaviors or processes. Although it is marvelous to discontinue an old or outdated process, the responsible members of the organization will quickly remind you that the shift in expectations has to be communicated across the organization and, if the process to be stopped has a high degree of interdependence, it should be discontinued at the appropriate time with involvement of others throughout the organization.

Establishing Transition Management Process

Although the existing management structures must begin working and "owning" this change, it is a mistake to depend completely on the existing structure for implementation. Supplement it by developing and establishing a process for overall management of transition planning, approval of recommendations, and reconciliation of the individual plans to make sure that they are synchronized and aligned. In large change efforts, it is common to dedicate people solely to managing the transition. In a participative structure, they will literally support others in transitioning their work, *not* do the transition work for them. Determining the role and function of the transition management is always an important decision, both in terms of how the overall effort is managed and of how the individuals and work groups are supported.

Establishing Integration Processes and Issue Resolution Forums

The work necessary to integrate a change into a large organization can be massive. It is likely there will be more processes working concurrently than previously and that the frequency with which they operate will greatly increase. As the design work progresses and work-unit design begins, there will be many issues that have to be resolved for the entire organization. These issues are now raised and turned into actions. This is often an extension or re-framing of the forum that has operated throughout the design process. Its purpose remains the same (to air and discuss issues), but the deliberations will become more detailed and require a different level of expertise. You must now identify the people to do the deliberations.

Identifying Individuals or Teams to Complete the Work

Identify task teams or individuals who will address the issues to be resolved, designs to be completed, and transition planning required. The individuals and task teams should do the following:

- Clarify the item or need

- Obtain approval for their approach from a designated change leader

- Accomplish their responsibilities

- Coordinate the impact of proposed resolutions, designs, or plans with stakeholders or other task teams that will be affected

- Obtain approvals, authorization, and buy-in as needed to proceed with implementation and transition

Summary

Task VII has taken the provisional design and moved it to the level of an implementation plan. The major outputs are these:

- A validated design

- Identification of further design work

- Timelines for design work

- A transition management process

- Integration processes and issue resolution forums

- Individuals or teams to complete the work

By this time, the organization will see changes in its role network. The amount of process support will be greatly increased as more parts of the organization are deeply impacted by the change. The number of change agents will also increase. The work of change will be shifting into the organization. As the change grows exponentially, it can quickly go beyond the ability of a leadership team or design team to monitor and track. Staying abreast of the change will require a closer monitoring of system performance as well as project planning. This leads to the work of Task VIII.

Points to Remember

Model the Design Intent with Implementation Approaches. Implementation and design completion must model the new design. Building your plans around the future state is a subtle but powerful enabler of change.

Continue to Support the Process. During implementation, leaders must recognize that there is still a lot of planning and design work to be done. It is important that they continue to support the process as they did earlier.

Recognize That Dialogue Is Increasingly Important. As the work-unit design begins, there will be an increasing number of questions and considerations. Dialogue around the intent of the design is the only way to resolve these, so plan on more time rather than less.

Determine Minimum Critical Specs. As the design moves to implementation, carry only what is critical to the intent of the work-unit design. No more, no less!

Common Trip Points

Moving to Deployment. View this step as one of expanding the design, not of deploying the answers.

Overplanning for Others. There is always an element of planning for others in a change effort. It is easy here to plan the rest of the effort immediately for everyone in the organization. But people must be allowed to plan for themselves as much as possible.

Becoming a Re-Staffing Exercise. There is typically some amount of job shuffling after a major change effort. Avoid turning the effort into a major staffing exercise now with the intent of getting the "right people" to enable the change. Bringing in new people at this point is both a limiter and a liberator. Although they may not be vested in the current state, they probably are not vested in the future state either. New people will still have to go through the work of the earlier tasks to become grounded in the effort.

Reducing Participation. As the work-unit design begins, the level of participation in the overall effort must move to a higher level. Don't revert to the traditional hierarchy of the organization to implement the change.

Assuming Work Units Can Complete Designs Without Support. Let's face it: Most organizations don't have many extra people, and the ones they have are usually quite busy. Taking on an extra piece of work, such as redesigning a work unit, is sometimes more than a group can comfortably do alone. Sometimes all it takes is an extra person to help out during design sessions or to stand in while unit members are off their normal jobs. Whatever it takes, it is worth identifying the need and committing to fill it.

Losing Sight of Design Intent. Even in high-participation change efforts, there will be people who have not been paying a lot of attention to what is happening or to the implications for the design. Unfortunately, these people are often in key leadership and control positions. As people begin to implement changes, they often become more focused on the mark they would like to make than on the overall intent of the design.

Losing Change Leadership. Even though the design is set, the need for change leadership remains high and expands through the organization. Many change leaders see their work as finished once the work moves into the realm of implementation. It's not over—it has only begun!

8

Task VIII: Establishing Metrics

The work of the Ten Tasks to this point has been in determining the organization's direction and the required structural elements to achieve its mission. In Task VIII, you begin to build the monitoring system to enable the performance of the new system. Metrics can be a strong force for moving toward the desired future; they can also, however, be used to maintain the organization as it is. Trying to change an organization without altering the existing metrics can be an exercise in futility. A well-designed metric system will be grounded in the performances that are necessary for the organization's purpose and supportive of its new direction.

The Work of Task VIII

High-performing organizations are built on the principle of having response-able people. These people need a continual stream of information to act in a timely and meaningful manner. The goal of this task is to establish metrics that provide people with critical information aligned with the strategic intent of the new design. This information may include feedback about the organization's culture and its levels of participation and collaboration. There is one other important consideration for this system: The system must be sufficiently fast and timely to meet the requirements of the overall business.

The scope of work for Task VIII will vary according to the nature and size of the change. The initial decision will be how extensive the system should be. It may only focus on a few key elements of the change, or it could be a completely new system in itself. The critical features to include are those that are most important to the new design. These features come directly from the work of Tasks V and VI in defining the purpose and boundaries of the work system and the intent of the design. This task has eleven major pieces of work:

- Determining the focus of the metrics
- Identifying the organization's learning need from the system
- Identifying the organization's levels of output
- Identifying categories of performance
- Identifying realistic metrics for categories
- Reinforcing appropriate behaviors
- Setting the scope of the metrics
- Determining data collection and analysis methods
- Determining format, feedback, and evaluation processes
- Agreeing on level of standardization
- Establishing a linkage to reward systems

Determining the Focus of the Metrics

A metric is intended to be used as a reflective tool and so should reflect what is important to the organization. The work of Task VI provided detailed information about what was important for the organization, both internally and externally. You should use the output requirements for each process thread identified in Task V as a basis for designing your metrics. When you begin to write the metrics, it will become fairly clear how well the work was done during earlier tasks. If the organization's purpose was clearly defined, setting the metric is fairly easy.

For instance, if the organization's purpose is to be the premier provider of a packaged good to a certain market segment, then the primary focus of the metric system should be how close the organization is coming to accomplishing that end. The system would draw focus to how well the packaged good is being provided, what the customers in the market segment think of that service, and how close the organization is to being premier. That's fairly straightforward so far. The next item to consider is the three fundamental areas of work—business, process, and people. When looking at the overall metric system, you should be able to see how each of these areas is working and find some sense of how well they are being jointly optimized.

One of the difficulties of constructing meaningful metric systems is that there are many important attributes of the organization and many interested stakeholders. Deciding what information must go to whom is an exercise in balance. In addition to balancing stakeholder needs, there is the issue of different needs and desires of others in the organization. You will often see metric systems that are primarily focused on accountability for the members. This approach is used when the primary objective of the creators of the system is to know whether people in the system are doing what they are supposed to be doing. Although this is important, you must remember that it is not the only use of a metric system. In deciding the balance, you must consider how much attention the system has to devote to this accountability, as opposed to how the process is working and how successful the overall system is at the time. Remember when making this choice that the goal of change is to increase performance. Build a system that supports performance.

Identifying the Organization's Learning Needs

The metric, being a reflective tool, will naturally guide the organization toward whatever it emphasizes. If the system focuses on errors, then the organization will learn about its errors. If it focuses on successes, then the organization will learn about its successes. If the system is exclusively directed toward the status quo, then it will promote a more singular view of success—and potentially miss emerging opportunities. On the other hand, a focus on opportunities will make it easier to shift, but it could also tend to diffuse the focus on the current processes of the organization. The key is to use the system as a learning device that supports important findings for the organization.

Adaptability as an organization is a function both of the ability to decide and take action and of the ability to scan and assimilate relevant information. With this in mind, building a metric system allows large parts of the organization to work at assimilation in a consistent manner and promotes overall organizational learning. The caution is that it is easy to build a system that, in the interest of speed and efficiency, supports the learning of only a few people. To best deal with the situation and to create the most useful metric system, first answer the following questions about the overall purpose of the system:

- Where will the information go and who will use it?

- How is it to be used and for what purposes?

The overall process of the system must include capturing the data, creating the metrics, and moving that information across organizational boundaries. In planning the flow, many organizations will funnel the information into the hands of a few people, such as an analyst or a supervisor, with the intention of shortening the process and speeding the flow. The downside to this is that all the learning from that information is focused on the analyst or supervisor, rather than on the person or people who use that information to do the work, which can, in turn, slow organizational growth and adaptability.

Identifying the Organization's Levels of Output

All organizations can be thought of as having multiple levels of output. For example, meaningful divisions can be at the work-unit level, at the department level, and at the overall organization level. Large organizations can have many such divisions. The overall metric system must make sense based on the level of organizational output(s) that it is intended to support. A typical error is to try to use organizational metrics at a work-unit level and attempt to guide action from them. It is often a frustrating or impossible task to try to figure out what impact the work unit has at the organization level in a time frame that you can actually work with. Organizational metrics often include financial items that are difficult to tie to a work-unit perspective. For example, consider return on investment. At a work-unit level, only work units whose core work is in managing this item can actually use this to drive meaningful action. The focus of the metric for the work unit should be on the item that is controllable at that level. Overall organization metrics should reflect the outcome of the collective actions of all the members of the organization.

Identifying Categories of Performance

Every organization can be divided into categories of performance. At the organization level, these may appear fairly consistent from organization to organization. In a corporate setting, many organizations would share the category of "financial." Other categories might include product innovation, market share, and customer satisfaction. As you move further into department or work units, the differences become more pronounced due to organization and process differences.

The important performance categories defined in Tasks I and V are usually determined by understanding the environment of the organization. They tend to relate to the stakeholders. These could be customer satisfaction, environmental impact, business development, product development cycle time, or regulatory compliance. At issue is whether there should be an ongoing system to monitor each aspect. Again, selection of these categories has a great deal of impact, both on the "face" of the organization and on its subsequent development. Strive to use enough categories to give a complete picture of what is important and few enough to keep it meaningful.

Identifying Realistic Metrics for Categories

If ever there were an appropriate place to say "Easier said than done," this is it. Within every category there will be a number of potentially enticing areas that lend themselves to metrics. Obtaining the right number and focus for this can be a real trick. First, be sure that the metric actually illustrates the category, moves in a proper time frame, and does so in a way recognizable to the members of the organization. Second, spend time with what may seem like semantics, but can be powerful shaping devices for ongoing growth of the organization.

Besides simply operationalizing important performance indicators, this also becomes a statement of how the creators of the metrics view the organization. A manufacturing site interested in the quality of its products might choose indicators such as "pounds of scrap" or "non-prime production." A site interested in the safety of its employees might choose "number of accidents" or "number of safety violations." Although these are important and are valid indicators of conditions in the organization, they also focus attention on undesirable events. These could be stated as "percent of prime production" or "number of safe hours worked" and still give the same information. Either way they are worded, they serve as a constant reminder and reinforcement of what is important in the organization. To the greatest extent possible, these should be worded to reflect the desired outcomes rather than the absence of them.

Another issue to consider is the level of performance that is reflected. A product development group could find a number of ways to monitor its performance and progress. If the focus is on group-level performance, they might track "number of products under development," "number of teams working," or "distribution of resources per project." A shift in emphasis to a higher organization level might lead that group to track "time to market," "product acceptance rates," or "existing product replacement rates." The challenge here is to focus on what makes the organization successful in its environment yet maintain enough internal focus to guide immediate action. Another consideration here is the time horizon. Many of the overall success factors require longer time frames. A work-unit level success factor has to have a shorter time horizon so groups can quickly adapt to market requirements. When designing metrics, try to strike a balance between these levels.

Reinforcing Appropriate Behaviors

Although the metric system is grounded in overall organization performance and success, it is enabled through individual behaviors. The indicators chosen should support the desired behaviors. All too often, the actual behaviors reinforced are less important or, worse, irrelevant to the overall system success. As this effort began, we framed the importance of collective intention. The first change processes were dialogues that began to clarify that intention.

The metric system should reflect that collective intention. When people look at and respond to these metrics, the action guided should be consistent with the intended outcome agreed to in the work of design. This exercise requires that you take a look at the overall vision and strategy and determine what important elements support the intention. The subsequent metrics must reflect that intention.

Setting the Scope of the Metrics

Another important decision when setting your assessment system is the overall scope. There is always a need to begin looking at what is happening immediately outside of a work group, but the question becomes, "How far outside?" The further from the day-to-day operation a system can take your thinking and reflection, the more it is likely to produce change and adaptation. The downside is in determining how you should appropriately respond to the information you receive.

In process-based organizations, this question is directed first in customer/supplier terms. How far ahead of your process boundary should your metric system look? Is there pertinent information there? Do you include information about the work units supplying your work input? Or an even larger question: Do you go outside the organization also? Do you include information about supplier alliances, including profitability? It can be very valuable to include supplier production rates and quality information.

Determining Data Collection and Analysis Methods

Work systems tend to generate large amounts of data. From a change perspective it is important that the data come from meaningful sources that are recognizable to the people who are working in the system. Data collection must be as easy, straightforward, and automatic as possible. The most powerful place for data collection and validation is in the hands of the people in the work group. Data kept in one part of a process about another is often useful only in creating divisiveness and defensiveness among the people in the organization.

After data have been collected and validated, some sort of initial analysis has to be performed. This can be as simple as the basic math required to determine units per hour or acceptance rates. The question for work groups is: "Who does it?" Is this the work of an expert or of someone outside the work group? Does the supervisor perform this work? Does any learning take place at this point? If there are assumptions that are applied in the analysis or if the analysis has a subjective nature, then it becomes more important to be explicit for the work group and to be clear about the method used. It is very important for people to recognize their data and understand how it is being used.

Determining Format, Feedback, and Evaluation Processes

Once the data are analyzed, the resultant information must make its way back to the people who have to act. Determining the format of the report is seemingly a fairly straightforward decision, but one must consider convenience and usability. At this point, simpler and faster is better. Data-based decisions about processes have to be as easy to make as possible. If the data is too hard to obtain or too slow in coming, there will be a lower probability that it will actually be used. Also, if data are not readily available, people will learn to act without it.

While the data are being evaluated, decisions or judgments about the overall process are made. Action typically ensues from this point, so it is easy to inadvertently short-circuit the learning process. In many organizations, the supervisor or manager will evaluate the data, typically in private, then publish the actions determined from his or her evaluation. On the surface this appears to be the most expedient method, but it actually slows down implementation when people are asked to take action without knowing the decision process behind the request. A more sustainable system is one in which the information is fed back to the people who are being asked to act and then an evaluation is done as collaboratively as possible.

Agreeing on Level of Standardization

Looking at the overall metric system, it is easy to see that it can become quite large. It can also quickly lose its relevance when there is too much information that cannot be tied to the work unit or when there is too much information to be absorbed quickly. One other potential trip wire is in over-specifying format and usage. It is important for each work group to receive the information that it needs—quickly and easily. But it is more important that the overall intent of the metric system be consistent throughout the organization than to have the actual system be consistent. Work units require flexibility to monitor what is important in the moment and to change their focus as needed. Organizations need stability in monitoring to make comparative decisions or meaningful reports to stakeholders and investors. Finding a balance about what is important throughout the system is critical.

Establishing Linkage to Reward System

Well-designed metric systems illuminate the process as it is—successes, failures, delays, and all—and provide accurate and timely information on system performance. Part of the design should address how performance can be attributed to the actions of individuals or groups in the organization and how the metrics will be tied to the reward system.

Be aware that people will make a linkage whether there is one or not. By that, we mean that if people are watching a metric system and are firmly grounded in the system performance, they will have an idea of what their contribution is and will compare that to their reward system. At some level, this will influence behavior of the members of the organization.

A metric system says a lot about the organization to a lot of people. The messages are not always clear and consistent, and they are not always interpreted in positive and constructive ways. The main point of a metric system should be in its ability to promote growth and adaptability. The information coming from the system must be reliable and be trusted by those making decisions. It must be responsive enough to sustain the findings of the people in the system, and it must be current enough to drive immediate action. There are many implications to what you choose to monitor, so make that choice well. With good analysis and input, it will go far toward building a meaningful system. Use Exhibit 8.1 as a checklist of questions for thinking through a metric system.

Summary

This task has taken the new system and has formalized the areas of focus across the organization. These are the major outputs:

- A set of metrics that balances the performance domains of the organization, for example, balancing operational efficiency with rapid product development

- Agreement on the level of focus for organization performance

- Structure and process for information collection and dissemination

- Requirements of the overall system for use in work-unit design completion

The metric system in itself will serve as the reflective tool for the overall organization and the desired future as a result of the change. It will provide the information required for each of the stakeholder groups and for the overall management of the system to monitor and improve performance. Remember, the meta-goal of change is high performance. The metric system should be designed to ensure that all parts of the organization are focused on what is important

Exhibit 8.1. Metrics Planning Questions.

Organization:	Primary Responsibility:
Stakeholder:	Support:

What is the focus of the metric system, specifically?	
Where will the information go and who will use it?	
How is it to be used and for what purposes?	
What system and individual behaviors is it intended to reinforce?	
What will be the scope of the assessment system?	
What levels of organizational output will it be tied to?	
What categories of performance will it address?	
What metrics will realistically illustrate the categories?	
How will data be collected and validated? How will it be analyzed?	
How will the information be formatted, fed back, and evaluated?	
How much of the process will be standard for the overall organization, and how much will be ad hoc to the individual work units?	
What will be the linkage to the reward system?	

and that the overall system truly reflects the performance of the whole system.

———————

Points to Remember

The System Is Built to Enable the Performer. The primary objective is to make sure that the people who are operating the system on a day-to-day basis are enabled by the information generated.

Information Is Funneled First to People Who Are Required to Act. The information generated should go first and primarily to the people whose responsibility it is to act. Going through a staff group or supervisor system may seem like a good idea, but it actually tends to slow down immediate action.

Focus on What You Want to Happen. The system must highlight the conditions, events, or outcomes that are important to the organization. As much as possible, avoid using a metric that describes the absence or avoidance of something (for example, "no dissatisfied customers").

Assimilation and Interpretation of the Data Is a Key Learning Activity. Taking the raw data and creating the information reflected in the metric is a learning activity. It should happen at the same point in the organization at which the process being measured is occurring, by the people who are controlling it. Doing otherwise limits people's learning and slows later adaptive change.

Metrics Reflect the Performance of the Whole System as Well as the Contribution of the Work Unit. Designing the metrics is a balance between designing for the whole system and for the work unit. The metrics must reflect the whole-system performance at the work-unit level, and the work-unit level must reflect in the whole-system performance. Ensure that the metrics you set reflect the total performance of all-important domains of the organization.

———————

Common Trip Points

Focusing Solely on Behaviors. Behaviors are important, but taken by themselves tend not to reflect overall performance.

Focusing Too Much on Accountability. Ensure that there is adequate balance between responsibility and accountability and that there is not an overreliance on accountability or making sure that people are "getting things done." A system built totally on accountability tends to drive all sorts of creative activity in the organization to make sure the numbers are right for next year's budget appropriation or performance review. These activities do not always add up to high performance of the organization.

Underestimating the Implementation and Change Work Required to Use the Metric System. Installing a completely new metric system, particularly if it has associated changes in management practice (such as compensation systems), can mean a large learning curve and require a great deal of time to implement. Be careful to balance the time between the learning effort and the expected implementation of the new system.

Misplacing Stakeholder Metrics. Although stakeholders want and need many things from a work system, not every part of the organization requires all of the information. The information might only serve as a distraction in some work units and could lead them away from their primary tasks.

Picking Measures That Are Too Slow to Drive Responsive Action. Many measures are only available on a yearly basis or are so slow coming back that they cannot be adjusted for before the product is out the door and in the customers' hands. Although these measures are important, be sure to include items that happen fast enough to impact the ongoing process.

Picking Metrics That Are Too Far from the Desired Consequences of the Work. If the metric reflects managerial approval more than quality of the work product, it may tend to drive behaviors that satisfy management, rather than enhance the performance of the overall organization. Choose carefully!

9

Task IX: Managing Transitions

By this stage in a change effort, if you have been following the Ten Tasks, much of the organization's population has been involved in one way or another. The last few months have probably been dedicated to establishing the new design, planning its implementation, and staffing it. The work to date has specified clearly what is necessary to preserve the integrity of the new system and set the minimum critical specifications for the organization. Now it is up to the people to work out the details in a way that brings the intended structures, processes, and cultural objectives into being.

The Work of Task IX

Most of the work of implementing the new designs and enabling the new business models will come naturally as the organization and its work units "get on with business." However, there is always the opportunity for divergence, and contingencies always arise while the organization is still in flux. In the early part of this transition phase, you will have to maintain a disciplined, well-organized process so that the transition doesn't "drift."

Because the actual people, responsibilities, structures, and processes vary from organization to organization and from work group to work group, this chapter simply presents sets of questions to be answered by the people in the specific situations. The objective is to stimulate thinking and collective discussion about issues that are important to the effective operation of a high-performing organization. People should discuss the issues from three interdependent perspectives: "How does this relate to the overall work system that my work unit is in?" "How does this relate to my specific work unit?" "How does this relate to me and my personal responsibilities, performance, and goals?"

Some of the questions in this chapter will be very relevant to particular jobs and work units; some may not be. Sometimes it will be important for a group to reach a common understanding on the issues raised; for other questions it may be less important. People will also have to add their own questions, rephrase what is asked, or set additional topics for discussion when appropriate. Some of the answers to the questions will have been addressed in whole or in part by the design effort to date. These answers must be provided to the people to help keep them on track. Most of the answers provided by the design will require further development. *All* of the material passed on from design will need creative decisions to apply it to the specifics of actual work situations.

Work groups must exercise judgment about how much effort to put into developing a common understanding and a group consensus on the answers to the questions in this chapter. They can tailor the material they cover, the issues they address, the timing and pacing of their transition work, and how they go about it. This will depend on how much design has already taken place at the work-unit level and how much change is being undertaken in the organization's structure and processes.

The goal of this task is to have people in the organization engage the change from a very practical level: "How do we make this work?" Every person's role is to make the overall system perform. This work should be approached as a new beginning with increased performance. Organization members will have to figure out how to address the required changes and how to open up the dialogues required to reach high performance. Remember that the goal is *high performance*, not just implementing a design.

The work of Task IX is broad and covers many areas of the organization. At this point, the change effort has reached all levels of the organization. Because of the speed of adaptation in organizations, work-unit design can easily go many different directions, so this task encompasses both guiding the overall change effort and completing a detailed design at all levels. There are four major pieces of work in this task:

- Maintaining constancy of purpose and positive strategic intent

- Defining work-unit skills, knowledge, and leadership requirements and planning the distribution among the roles

- Establishing decision slopes with each work unit and planning the requirements and pacing of the transitions

- Planning and supporting the development of individual abilities

Maintaining Constancy of Purpose and Positive Strategic Intent

In Task VII you established a communication network to handle integration of the design completion activities. The people in the network's job is to ensure

- That the people and work groups of the organization have the information and support they require to work through the details of implementation

- That the details being worked out at the individual work-unit and organization levels remain true to the intent of the overall design

- That the timing and pacing of implementation activities stay in sync across the organization

- That cross-boundary processes remain integrated

- That issues that emerge during implementation planning and transition that are not being worked out through established organizational processes are identified and prioritized

- That follow-up responsibilities for resolution are assigned

By Task IX, the work of the change is becoming the work of the organization. One key concept of change management is that implementation is always the responsibility of the people who will ultimately be doing the work. The transition network is there to ensure that the new system is properly integrated between the work units. Although many change efforts deploy changes from the top down, the Ten Tasks maintain the iterative nature of organizations. Thus, changes at the work-unit level will always have to be reflected and tested against the overall design intent to maintain constancy of purpose.

As you move into work system design, there is always the opportunity to drift. For example, on a previous project on which we worked, we had completed the provisional design and begun implementing steps to complete the design through a process involving everyone in the company. During the initial implementation, the broad participation in this phase created changes to the design that were inconsistent with the fundamental design principles. Most of these "interventions" were by leadership holding on to certain "sacred cows," with others emerging due to a different understanding of the basic design.

Two years later, we reviewed progress toward realizing the design vision. We formed a team to compare the current state with the basic design. Following this study, we made changes to the organization that (1) implemented those features not originally implemented; (2) adjusted the organization to reverse the "interventions"; and (3) made additional improvements consistent with the original design principles. Several factors may have helped us to regain the ground apparently lost:

- The original design work used an open process

- A "critical mass" of employees understood the principles and championed the vision over the two-year period

- It was openly recognized that the provisional design had not been fully implemented

- There had been relentless communication of the vision

- Top leadership fully supported the new design

Defining Work-Unit Requirements

The Organization Wheel, described in the first chapter of this book and shown again in Figure 9.1, represents a work system view of an organization. For any change in one of the elements around The Wheel to "stick," relevant changes in other elements must take place. In an ongoing work system, the need for change can arise in any of the elements of The Wheel, and the task becomes to accommodate the change and to bring the system back into balance.

Although questions in this chapter are framed for implementation of the new designs at the work group level, they can also be applied to larger organization business units and to the overall organization.

When you first view the list of questions to be answered, it can appear daunting. We have seen situations in which one person takes the list of questions and answers them for the other members of the work unit. While that does answer the questions, it will do little to finish the task. The objective is to create a set of working agreements based on the design intent of the change. That requires dialogue and agreement. In many cases it may not even be necessary

Figure 9.1. The Organization Wheel.

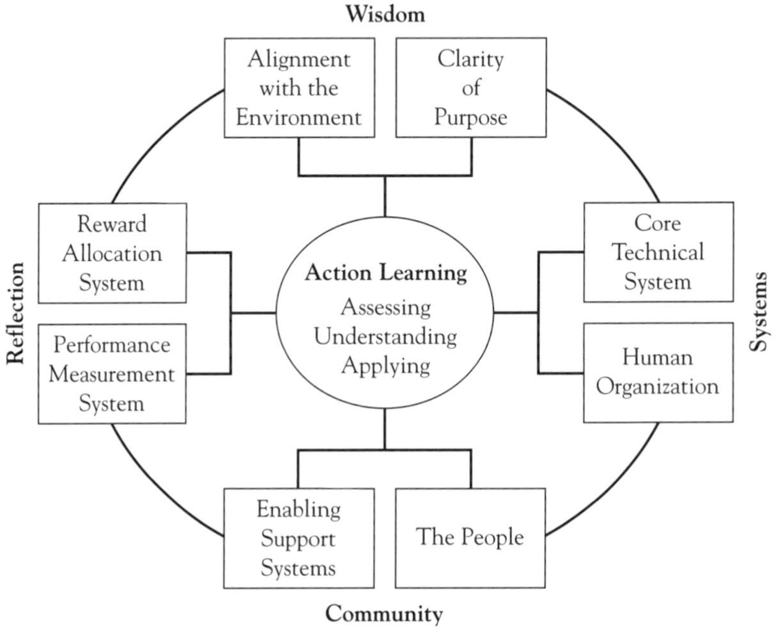

Wisdom

Reflection

```
        ┌──────────────┐  ┌──────────────┐
        │  Alignment   │  │   Clarity    │
        │  with the    │  │     of       │
        │ Environment  │  │   Purpose    │
        └──────────────┘  └──────────────┘

┌──────────────┐                        ┌──────────────┐
│   Reward     │      Action Learning   │     Core     │
│  Allocation  │                        │  Technical   │
│   System     │      Assessing         │   System     │
└──────────────┘      Understanding     └──────────────┘
┌──────────────┐      Applying          ┌──────────────┐
│ Performance  │                        │    Human     │
│ Measurement  │                        │ Organization │
│   System     │                        └──────────────┘
└──────────────┘

        ┌──────────────┐  ┌──────────────┐
        │   Enabling   │  │              │
        │   Support    │  │  The People  │
        │   Systems    │  │              │
        └──────────────┘  └──────────────┘
```

Systems

Community

to document the responses. Many of the items can be covered in a quick conversation among co-workers. The ultimate repository for answers is in the collective heads and hearts of the people doing the work. Remember, documents do not change organizations, people's actions do.

Addressing the Elements of The Wheel

Before heading into the first element of The Wheel, revisit the organization's design intentions and minimum critical specifications. This is a transition to a well-thought-through and integrated design, not starting over from scratch and trying to reinvent the world from your work group's point of view. Before answering the questions, read through the entire chapter quickly to get an overall sense of what has to be accomplished.

Alignment with the Environment

This element deals with the things outside of your work unit's boundaries that impact what you do and how you do it. By definition, something outside of your boundaries is outside of your control. You may be able to influence these things, but you cannot dictate them. Critical to your success is an awareness of such things as the trends and dynamics in your environment, the requirements of your customers, the expectations of your key stakeholders, and the demands of the larger work system.

The Larger Work System

- What is the parent organization's major business process (as outlined in Task VI) and how is it supposed to work?

- What are the minimum critical specifications for the overall organization and your work unit?

- What are the critical success factors for the overall organization and your work unit?

Customers

- Who are the direct customers of your work unit's core processes?

- What products do they receive from you, and what are their service expectations of you?

- What are your expectations of them?

- How will your transactions and your coordination with them take place?

Suppliers

- Who are your direct suppliers of "core process" input?

- Where does your important process, planning, coordination, and control information come from?

- What are your expectations of your suppliers regarding input and information, and what are their expectations of you?

- How will your transactions and your coordination with your suppliers of input and information take place?

Regulators

- What organizational groups, industry or governmental agencies, communities or community action groups, and so forth have important expectations about what you do or how you go about it?

- What are their expectations of you?

- How do you plan to deal with them?

Investors and Upper Level Management

- What are investors' and upper management's expectations about what you do and how you go about it?

- How are they communicated to you?

- How do you plan to deal with them?

Dynamics and Trends

- What dynamics and trends in the environment may be important for your work unit to understand and track?

- How might you best track the most important dynamics and trends?

- What actions do you need to take to set up these information-gathering and processing capabilities?

Clarity of Purpose

This element deals with your sense of who you are, what you intend to be, and how you will get there. It deals with your common agreement on mission, vision, values, and plans; how well these things are understood across your work system; and how influential they are in guiding the actions of your organization's members in their day-to-day work.

Mission and Vision

- What is the mission of this work unit, and what is your vision of excellence for it?

- What are the critical success factors for accomplishing your mission and realizing your vision?

- How important is it for these things to be understood across your work system, and how influential should they be in guiding the actions of your organization's members in their day-to-day work?

Operating Philosophy

- What core values (business, process, and QWL) are represented in your vision?

- How is this work unit intended to operate culturally?

- How important is it for these things to be understood across your work system, and how influential should they be in guiding the actions of your organization's members in their day-to-day work?

Strategies

- What are your strategies for achieving the critical success factors you have identified?

- What voids in strategy exist that have to be explored further?

- How important is it for these things to be understood across your work system, and how influential should they be in guiding the actions of your organization's members in their day-to-day work?

Business Planning

- How will your strategies be executed?

- What processes will be required to plan your work unit's operation on a continuing basis?

- How important is it for these things to be understood across your work system, and how influential should they be in guiding the actions of your organization's members in their day-to-day work?

Support Needs

- What support is needed to maintain this clarity of purpose?

- Where do you expect this support to come from?

Core Technical System

This element deals with the processes that produce the core products and services of your work unit, the critical variables in those processes that you must stay on top of, and the information, knowledge, skills, and capabilities required.

Your Core Process(es)

- What are the core products of this work unit, who are the customers, and what are their critical specifications for the products?

- What are the inputs required to produce your core products, and where do they come from?

- What are the major stages of development of each of your core products? What are the major interim state changes during your core products' transformation from input to final output?

- What work has to be done to accomplish and manage each stage in the transformation process, and how does the work flow?

- What issues have to be deliberated, who becomes involved, and how are decisions set?

- What can go wrong (or what absolutely has to go right) in the core process(es) that can materially affect the important qualities of your product? That is, what are the critical variables in the process that you will have to keep in focus to complete your mission? (These are good candidates for measurement for process control.)

Information Needs

- What information is required to accomplish your core processes and manage the important variables?

- Where do you expect this information to come from?

- What will you have to do to reach the timing, pacing, and quality of service that you feel is required to achieve your mission?

Support Needs

- What support is needed to accomplish your core processes and manage the important variables?

- Where do you expect this support to come from?

- What will you have to do to reach the timing, pacing, and quality of service that you feel is required to achieve your mission?

Skills, Knowledge, and Capabilities

- What are the skills, knowledge, and capabilities required to accomplish the work identified for this element?

Human Organization

This element encompasses the role and authority structure of your organization and the network of human interactions and relationships required to define its work, coordinate its activities, and deal with its environment.

Distribution of Roles and Responsibilities

- What role structure and operating principles are defined for this work unit?

- What kinds of work are required by this work unit?

  To accomplish the core processes and control process variables at their source?

  To plan and coordinate efforts within the work unit and within the environment?

  To accomplish the overall mission?

  To track performance and seek continuous improvement?

  To handle contingencies and prepare for the future?

- What distribution of skills, knowledge, and abilities is needed within this role structure to accomplish this work in a way that jointly achieves business, operating, and QWL objectives?

  Entry skills for your work unit?

  Skills everybody must have?

Specialty skills: How many people should have each? Who?

What skill areas beyond the strict needs of the work unit offer opportunity for personal enrichment?

- From day-to-day and longer term, how will the work to be accomplished by this work unit be identified, defined, prioritized, scheduled, and allocated to the various members?

- What access and authority to commit the resources of this work unit are needed to accomplish the work processes, coordinate with the environment, and plan for the future (near term and longer term)?

Team Process

- How will the individual members of this work unit relate to one another in their day-to-day work?

- How will the overall work unit administration and support responsibilities be handled?

- How will the work of the individual members be coordinated?

- How will contingencies and problems be handled?

- How will decisions be made?

- How will information be shared and capabilities be developed among the members of this work unit?

- How will interfaces be handled across work-unit boundaries?

- What are the opportunities for self-direction and shared leadership within this work unit?

Team Process Development

- What team process capabilities does your work unit already have?

- What additional team process capabilities does your work unit need?

- How much development of the needed additional team process capabilities can be handled by resources internal to your work unit? How much will require support from learning and development resources external to your work unit?

- How will the development of the needed additional team process capabilities be planned and accomplished within the work unit?

- How will team process development support be planned, acquired, and coordinated with learning and development resources external to the work unit?

Team Agreements

- What behaviors do the members of this work unit have to exhibit?

  In how you conduct yourselves and how you represent your work unit in dealings with customers, associates, suppliers, and other stakeholders?

  In your approach to your work, your responsibilities, and stewardship of your resources?

  When you work together on common tasks or commitments you have made to one another regarding your work?

  In your general working relationships with one another, in your treatment of each other as members of this work unit, and in your treatment of each other and yourselves as diverse human beings?

- How will you establish your team's "contract" to live up to team agreements?

- How will you provide feedback to one another on the behaviors you exhibit?

- What will be your process for identifying and working through issues related to your team agreements as they arise?

- How will you update these agreements as you continue to work your way around The Wheel and proceed on with your business?

The People

This element deals with the four "C's" of people in organization: capabilities, culture, career expectations, and character. It addresses the match between these characteristics and the needs of the system, identifying places where you will have to make adjustments to your system or establish developmental plans for people.

Capabilities and Needs for Development

- What is the present distribution of existing abilities among the members of your work unit?

- How does it match up with your work unit's plan for skills distribution?

- What developmental needs do you have within your work unit?

- How much of the development can be handled by resources internal to your work unit? How much will require support from resources external to your work unit?

- How will the development be planned and coordinated within the work unit and with development resources external to the work unit?

- What actions do you have to take to set this up? (Further discussion of this question is part of the *Support Systems* element to follow.)

Culture: What You Have Learned in Common and How You Act on It

- What are the implications of a new culture for your work unit reflected in the work accomplished with the elements of The Wheel so far?

- What are the key attributes of the new culture, and what behaviors would reflect them (individual and team)?

- How are these behaviors similar to or different from the behaviors in your culture up to this time?

- What are the "reinforcements" in your environment that will either support or deter the desired behaviors?

- How can you capitalize on the positive and minimize the negative reinforcement?

- How can you reinforce behaviors in your environment that are important to your success and prosperity?

- What actions do you have to take to accomplish this?

Careers and QWL Enhancement Opportunities

- What is your QWL experience to date, and in what ways can it be enhanced in the future?

- What are the important future QWL goals of each of your work-unit members?

- What quality-of-work-life enhancement opportunities do you have under your control within this work unit?

- What can you do to jointly optimize your business objectives, your vision of excellence in operations, and your QWL goals?

- What actions do you have to take within your work unit to further your objectives?

- What cooperation do you require from your environment to achieve your objectives?

- What actions do you have to take to secure this cooperation?

- What things are so far out of your influence and control that you have to learn to live with them gracefully? (Are you *really sure* they are that far out of your influence and control?)

Character and the Diverse Basic Nature of Your People

- What must you do in your work unit to inspire peak performance?

- What can you personally do to inspire your own peak performance?

- What support do you want from the other members of this work unit to achieve your goals?

- What support and cooperation do you require from outside your work unit?

- What actions do you have to take to obtain the desired support?

Support Systems

There is a great deal of other work required by your work unit beyond that directly involved with the core transformation processes. This element deals with the processes that provide this technical support work, human administration support work, and the "boundary management" work involved in adapting to present contingencies and the evolving future.

Internal Support

- What support does your work unit require in any of the following areas, and how will you get it?

  Information

  Data management

  Documentation services

  Customer contact or service

  Supplier relations

  Purchasing

  Shipping and receiving

  Accounting, finance, budget

  Material control

  Equipment maintenance, calibration

  Technical support

  Safety, health, environmental

  Administrative support

  Others

- Will management of support processes be distributed across the work unit or contained in the jobs of a person or subgroup?

Integration and Coordination Across
Work-Unit Boundaries

- Given the support requirements established here, what outside groups might provide that support better than if you handle it within the work unit?

- What sort of partnerships should be established with other work units to fulfill your support requirements?

- What action do you have to take to secure these partnerships?

- What action do you have to take to coordinate with these groups?

Performance Measurement

This element deals with the performance measurement system to obtain status and trends in the business, technical processes, and human activity required to accomplish the work and meet the objectives of the organization. This is the work-unit detail that complements and enhances the overall system metrics established in Task VIII.

Objectives of Measurement

- What is the purpose of the overall assessment system designed in Task VIII?

- Where will the information go, and who will use it?

- How is it to be used and for what purposes?

- How will it be linked to the reward system?

Focus of Measurement

- What business, process, and individual behavior is the performance measurement system intended to reinforce?

- What will be the scope of the measurements?

- What levels of organizational output will it track (overall business, business process, organization, work unit,
  team, individual, and so forth)?

Content of the Measures

- What categories of performance will be addressed?

- What will be the weighting among the categories?

- What metrics will realistically illustrate the categories?

Assessment Process

- How will data be collected and validated?

- How will it be analyzed?

- How will the information be formatted, fed back, and
  evaluated?

- How much of the process will be standard and tied to
  an assessment system for the overall organization, and
  how much will be ad hoc to this individual work unit?

Reward Allocation

This element deals with the range of rewards available for participation in the organization and the best way to allocate them in
order to reinforce the critical performance characteristics you have
identified.

Objectives and Nature of the Reward System

- How does your present pay and promotion system support or deter the critical business, systems, and human
  performance requirements identified so far?

- What other opportunities for reward are internally
  available to your work unit? (Remember that "reward"
  is in the eye of the beholder.)

- What opportunities for reward are available to you to use in reinforcing desired behaviors of your work unit's external stakeholders? (Again, remember that "reward" is in the eye of the beholder.)

- What will be the linkage between your reward system and your performance measurement system?

- What may have to change in the formal pay, promotion, and recognition system of your parent organization to support its critical business, systems, and human performance adequately?

- What may have to change in the informal reward and recognition habits in the culture of your parent organization to support its critical business, systems, and human performance adequately?

- What do you have to do to open up a dialogue about this?

Action Learning

This element addresses the processes, structures, and culture related to learning from your experiences and applying that learning for continuous improvement and renewal. The process involves cycles of gathering data from an experience, analyzing that data to develop a credible "story" of what happened, generalizing from the situation to update your "theories" about how things work, and then applying that learning in a new situation, and so on.

Your Learning Environment

- What are your organization's most significant strengths that you can build on for organizational learning?

- What are your organization's most significant barriers to organizational learning that you must address?

- What do the members of your work unit have to be

able to do to engage in the organizational and personal learning processes successfully?

Information

- What information should be regularly disseminated throughout your work system?

- How can you collectively interpret new information?

Performance Monitoring

- How can you collectively interpret the results of the work system's performance?

- How will you use work system performance information to learn and improve your processes?

- How will you analyze critical incidents in a way that will promote process improvement, rather than promote punishment for shortfalls?

Knowledge Systems

- How will you capture and share learning gained from your information and monitoring systems?

- What sort of access to this knowledge will be available?

Establishing Decision Slopes and Plan Transitions

Invariably, the work system design will uncover new skills and new responsibilities to enable. Sometimes the shift is quite dramatic and requires a good bit of time and development before all of the people can function within the new roles. Often, work was being performed by other work units or support organizations. This work often has to be supported by a skilled person until it can be handed off.

We use a "decision slope" like the one shown in Figure 9.2 to document the transition activities required. The goal is to understand who is doing what—and for how long. It is not a role distribution, but a planning activity that is intended to provide a smooth transition from the old work system to the new.

As Figure 9.2 demonstrates, there is a gradual shift into the new work required and a phase-out of the work of the old system. Every piece of work that is currently being done for some customer will have to be transitioned gracefully and supported well.

Planning and Supporting the Development of Individual Capabilities

The last piece, and possibly the most important, is to provide for and support the required development of the people within the system. This work should be grounded in the requirements detailed in the work-unit design as well as the overall organization design. The work system will only perform as well as the people within it. Help them become world class.

Figure 9.2. The Decision Slope.

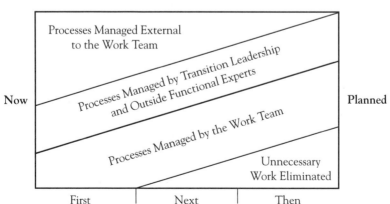

Summary

The work of this task covers all levels of the organization and involves completing the design down to the work-unit level. The overarching work is in maintaining the overall intention of the design while unfolding the change across the organization by encouraging creativity in work-unit design and providing necessary resources. The work you undertake in designing the overall strategic intents and the minimum critical specifications for the organization is critical.

Points to Remember

Ensure Positive and Strategic Focus. The energy of the effort has to be positive and strategic, as opposed to focusing on undoing or fixing the current state.

Maintain Joint Optimization. Remember that every aspect of the organization must be optimized within the business, process, and people dimensions.

Focus Design Completion at the Work-Unit Level. The last elements of design must be completed down to the work-unit level. Those design decisions should be made there and supported globally through the change effort and transition management structure.

Manage the Transition—Expect High Performance. During the transition effort, there may be a tendency to try to manage the results or impacts of the change. The results will come from the design. Stay focused on managing the transition itself and expect that high performance will ensue.

Common Trip Points

Losing Strategic Intent. Because the effort spreads into so many small corners of the organization, it is easy to focus on the details of completion, rather than on the strategic intent of the design.

Focusing Solely on the Work Unit. Just as the business, technical, and human dimensions require joint optimization, the work unit must be optimized jointly with the larger organization and other interrelated work units. Focusing design completion at the individual work-unit level without regard for the larger organization will result in a suboptimal design.

Inadequate Attention to Skills Transition. Although the structural elements of the design will create the overall arena in which the change will occur, the day-to-day success will come from the skills of the people at the work-unit level. New skills requirements are a part of every change, and they must be addressed before you can hope to sustain the change.

10

Task X: Continuous Learning and Improvement

Learning is what organizations do, not something you have to *make* them do. Learning is the continuous process of an organization attempting to align itself with shifts in its marketplace and with the realities of its external financial, physical, social, political, and technological environment. It is the organization's drive to synchronize purpose, process, structures, people, information, rewards and management systems within itself and with an unintegrated outside world in which it lives. Sound familiar? That's because if you substitute the word "changing" for the word "learning" you have the opening of Chapter Zero. *Organization change is organizational learning.* Organizational learning is people in an organization collaboratively learning together, and change stewardship is guiding that collaborative learning process.

The Work of Task X

The work of Task X is to build the capacity for ongoing change into the organization. One of the things we learn by going through a large change process is how easy it is to bring about change when the organization is engaged and ready. In tomorrow's world (as well as today's), organizations will have to be agile and adaptable to survive in an increasingly dynamic and complex environment (Evans & Thach, 2000). The work of change stewardship continues well beyond a single change and becomes an ongoing part of organization capability. This work is in keeping the organization engaged and ready for change.

The good news is that the mechanisms required to do this are fairly simple and, by this time in your change effort, are already functioning in the organization. The networks and roles established in the early work of the Ten Tasks began as a way of focusing attention on the change that was planned for the organization. They now become a more or less permanent part of the organization, focused on maintaining adaptability. The outcome of Task X is a set of processes and structures for ongoing learning and improvement that emphasize action learning. This task has four major pieces of work:

- Understanding the organizational learning process

- Designing your organizational learning process thread

- Developing ongoing capability to support organizational learning

- Planning for closure and celebration

Understanding the Organizational Learning Process

The current change work has taught the organization a great deal about itself. The overall constellation of issues (some good, some bad) that began this effort will not go away, but will simply be replaced by a new constellation of issues (some good, some bad). Because of the work of understanding the environment and purpose, the issues should be, overall, less problematic than before. You can be assured, however, that the organization will continue to require alignment as the environment continues to change. Every organization has a natural learning process. Understanding that process and how to emphasize and enhance it is the work of Task X.

Human Learning

Human learning proceeds in a cycle of doing, experiencing, making sense out of the experience, and then doing it or something else again (Argyris & Schön, 1996; Kolb, 1976; Pfeiffer & Jones, 1980; Senge, 1990). In the cycle, we develop theories (our beliefs, attitudes, and values) about how things work and how we can or cannot affect them. The whirlwind spirals round and round, usually outside of our consciousness, lifting us upward, we hope to a larger and better knowledge base. Sometimes things don't happen the way we expect, so we either ignore the event or change our theories (Festinger, 1957, 1964). When we cannot make sense of what is happening and get stuck somewhere in the learning process, we often become anxious and retreat to an inner reality, or we search for a divine being who can control it better than we can, or we go into culture shock or go crazy or grow terrified and run like heck. In day-to-day life, we don't usually pay attention to the fact that we are learning unless someone we pay attention to tells us that our theories are screwed up or our experience of what actually happens isn't what we expected to happen. Then the spinning cycle slows down for us and we become aware, sometimes quite painfully, that we are in a learning situation.

The spiral we've been talking about is called *the learning cycle* and is illustrated by Figure 10.1. The picture is our version of a model commonly used in our field (Argyris & Schön, 1996; Rothwell, 1999; Senge 1990; Senge, Kleiner, Roberts, Ross, & Smith, 1994). The cycle is sometimes referred to as *action learning* or *discovery learning*.

In common use, the term "learning" usually just means a conscious activity in one or another of the quadrants of the cycle: (1) planning what to do next; (2) taking the action; (3) reflecting on what happened; and (4) generalizing what you found and updating your beliefs about yourself and the world around you.

Figure 10.1. The Learning Cycle.

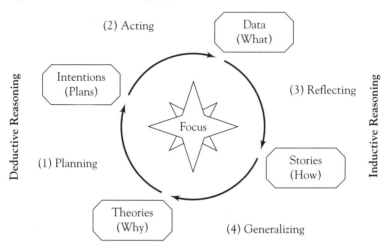

What you do in school, called "education," is mostly quadrant 4 work—learning theories based on other people's experiences. Newspapers, books, TV, and movies fill us with stories that enrich or twist our own story making in quadrant 3. Other people (imaginary or real) serve us as role models to copy actions from quadrant 2. Mentors give us advice and direction (directly, through media, or in our imagination), helping us do the planning in quadrant 1. However, we believe that there is no real learning without action and that responsible action is impossible without reflective internalization, that is, the whole cycle is what *learning* is all about.

Please note that, although we will present the cycle in a linear fashion, it is possible that events in any given quadrant may result in the learning backing up or even skipping ahead.

Let's begin exploring the cycle at the bottom of the figure, sitting in the box of theories—the "why" box of beliefs, attitudes, and values. Something catches our attention; that becomes the "focus" at the center of the cycle; and we are off to the races. It's that focus that makes this a coherent model. It directs our attention to a particular set of files in our theory box and will guide us in making sense out of what is going on in each of the quadrants. With that focus, we open our file drawer of theories and beliefs, sort through the jumble, pull out all the ones that seem to apply, and come up with an idea of where we would like to go and how we can get there. That's the transformation work of quadrant 1, labeled *planning*. This planning turns focuses and theories into intentions and plans. By the way, the happenings at any point around the cycle can also change the focus. If you are trying to analyze last year's production data so you can do a better job of forecasting supply needs, and you discover that the plant in Oxbow has been 20 percent off production goals for the last three quarters and nobody has bothered to tell you about it, I guarantee your focus will shift. In any event, after the transformation work of quadrant 1, we have a new state of information and knowledge called *intentions* and *plans*, together with a new or reaffirmed *focus*. The conversion process of quadrant 2, labeled *acting*, turns data from our experience of *what* happened into knowledge and information. Some of these data are tacit, measurable, codifiable, and recordable. Some are implicit, subjective, and heavily influenced by the beliefs we carry into the experience with us. Some are "thought" data, while others are "feeling" data. Some are conscious and some are buried in the non-conscious processing of our mind. In quadrant 3, *reflecting*, we pull out the data from our experience, match it against other experiences, and put together a coherent *story* of what happened. Human minds seem to do that no matter how big the holes in the *data* (Nevis, 1987). In quadrant 4, *generalizing*, we match the story against our files of beliefs, attitudes, and values, then generalize from the experience and either discount, validate, or update the *data*, the *story* or our *theories* or our *focus* (Rokeach, 1970). We are now once around the cycle with our files of theory, beliefs, attitudes, and values, ready for another focus to catch our learning attention.

Individual Learning Preferences

Some people pay more conscious attention to one part of the cycle than to another (Kolb, 1976). Remember last Thanksgiving when you missed the big family get-together, with all the aunts and uncles, cousins, and their spouses that you always go to? Remember the letters they sent you afterward to catch you up on the family gossip and say how much they missed you? First, there was Aunt Hattie's note. She always describes every detail, who arrived and when, what the overflowing table looked like, what Charlie said to Ruth, and every word of the fight between Sally and Jim. Great quadrant 3 stuff! Sarah covered the same things but, as you know, she always talks in little quadrant 4 theories such as: "Fred doesn't like to miss anything, so he and Emma came early," "Mom and Dad are trying to prove they don't need our help by still doing Thanksgiving and putting so much on the table," and "Sally and Jim are closer to a divorce than ever before." Down there in quadrant 1, John tells you that next year everyone should arrive a little earlier and at the same time so you could get a feel for what was going to happen at dinner and prepare yourself better. He wants to get together to figure out who is going to do dinner next year and how to approach Mom and Dad about it. He thinks Sally and Jim should start marriage counseling. Uncle Joe, our good old entrepreneur up in quadrant 2 with the two electrical stores and the refinished furniture business, doesn't write much but he did leave you a voice mail. He said his secretary is booking a restaurant for next year no matter what his sister and brother-in-law want to do. A friend who is a marriage counselor owes him a favor, so he has persuaded the guy to call Sally because he just isn't going to put up with the arguing any more. And by the way, "If you'd like, I can talk to your boss so you won't have to miss next year too!"

Sometimes it's people's nature to lean toward one strength or another; their nature frequently carries over in their work. There are the engineering groups turning principles into structures with little contact with the fruits of their labor—quadrant 1. Engineers traditionally start at the bottom of the cycle, with a challenge and the principles to be applied, then work their way up the left side with creative *deductive* reasoning to change the face of the globe. Scientists with disdain for principles they haven't personally coaxed from the data are typically found in quadrants 3 and 4. Scientists start at the top of the cycle with raw *data* and work their way *inductively* down the right side, quietly changing the world as they pursue their hobbies. For scientists, it's the raw *data* that they see as *information*; somebody else's propositions and theories just get in the way. For engineers, the *puzzle* to be solved and the *methods* to solve it are the information. *Data* isn't information unless it's from one of their own tests.

Then there is the sales representative struggling along in quadrant 2, trying one approach and getting rejected, going with another and getting rebuffed, trying something else and finally making a sale with little reflection on why each is happening and with little planning for the next client. There is the "idea generator" manager, living his working life in quadrant 1, who reads the memo, gets on the phone, barks out a few orders about how to fix the situation, and moves on to another issue in a kind of "ready, fire, aim" approach to accomplishment.

What is it they say? Reporters describe the flood. Scientists try to figure out why it caused so much damage. Congress calls in some engineering companies to estimate the cost of a dam. Meanwhile, the guy who seeded the clouds in the first place to see whether he could increase his corn crop has already sold the farm and is into mountain real estate in Colorado.

By the way, for the engineers among us, calling *planning* quadrant "1" makes perfect sense. On the other hand, the inductive learners reading this book are probably a little disturbed that we didn't call *reflection* quadrant "1."

Understanding Your Organization's Learning Style

Organizational learning follows the same path as individual learning, so after the people working on the Ten Tasks have an adequate understanding of the human learning cycle, they will be in a position to begin exploring their own organization's learning style. Through the change effort, they will have encountered many cases where the learning worked really well, accelerating the process, and where it worked poorly, slowing the process. We approach these issues in working with organizations as places where the learning cycle may be blocked or interrupted. These blocks may be temporary or habitual, related to the parts of the *learning cycle* that the organization characteristically does not do well. These cultural issues can be the most problematic because the roadblocks are usually very well entrenched. This presents you with an organizational change challenge in itself, a mini-change project within a change project. Think it through with the Ten Tasks in mind. Use the experience you have acquired so far from the change to understand the learning process and your organization's change capability.

Getting Stuck in the Learning Process

In people's day-to-day living, most of the cycles are quick and unconscious and have to do with trivial things similar to getting across the street safely. The process becomes conscious only when it slows down because you are facing a really sticky puzzle, or when the experiential data doesn't match the intention, or if the story doesn't jive with the data, or if the theory doesn't match any of it, or you just can't turn intentions into actions. You suddenly realize that you are in a learning experience when you are stuck at some place in the cycle, flunking at the task. There are a host of dysfunctional things you can do at this time, mainly tied to confusing the feelings of learning with the feelings of failure. The three classic dysfunctional reactions are *flight* (just go away literally or mentally), *fight* (find someone or something to blame and beat up), or *pairing* (find someone to sympathize with your predicament and help you forget that it ever happened). Organizations do the same things.

In your work with the Ten Tasks, you will have encountered a lot of people and organizations stuck somewhere in the learning cycle. You will find them retreating into one of the classic avoidance modes when they should be rolling up their sleeves and getting down to work. Sometimes they can use a little help to figure out how they are stuck, why they are stuck, and what they can do to get unstuck. How to help them is the subject of the next section.

Designing Your Organizational Learning Process Thread

This piece of work builds a structure that formalizes the ability of your organization to grow and adapt to the environment through action learning. There are three items to consider:

- The experiences of learning during the change process to date

- The requirements to support your learning process, both from the environment and from your organization's key learning habits

- Attributes of organizational learning enablers

These elements will combine to form the focus and requirements for process thread analysis and design. The tools and techniques are the same as in Tasks V and VI; however, this process thread has a bit softer output. Building this process thread enables the organization to improve continuously through learning and also creates valid, ongoing work toward that end.

As we stated earlier, when the learning cycle is working well it is basically invisible. It is best highlighted when the organization is under stress and people begin to get stuck. Understanding how to start moving again is helpful in designing the process thread.

Helping People and Organizations Get Unstuck

You can use the *learning cycle* to diagnose how someone or an organization is stuck when things don't seem to be progressing. You can use the same logic you did when you analyzed business processes in Chapter Five to analyze how people, groups, or organizations are stuck in their learning cycles. Think about the cycle as a circular *process thread* with each arrow representing a change of state from one major milestone to the next, with the information states in the boxes at the intersection of the arrows. You can use that analysis approach to figure out what's going on, what the priority variables and priority controllable actions are, and what has to be done to keep the wheel turning. After all, inaction or inappropriate action comes from a breakdown of the cycle, not from stupidity or ignorance. For the individual, you can look objectively at the environmental or psychological characteristics that are influencing the process breakdown. For the organization, add the ideas about *human systems analysis* from Chapter Five. Then use the design ideas from Chapter Six to design a strategy to help start people moving again.

As an example, look at the upper-right quadrant, *reflecting*. Think of the arrow as a *process* transforming or converting *data* into *stories*. First, be clear about the wanted output—*stories*—and the input—*data*—required to produce them. Ask the following:

- What are people trying to learn about?
- To what purpose will they use their stories?
- Who are the customers and the other stakeholders in the learning?
- What are their expectations of the product at this stage in the cycle?

To answer those questions well, people have to be clear about their *focus*. How can you help them gain clarity? Once they are clear on their focus, do they have enough of the right data to build a reliable story? If not, why not? Maybe it isn't the work of this quadrant that has them stuck. Maybe they are stuck because the work of an earlier quadrant wasn't done adequately. If there is enough data, what are some of the things that could go wrong or have to go right for this process to go well? Some of the problems will have to do with errors or misrepresentations that can creep in as people build their *stories*. Some will have to do with discovering missing parts needed to build a whole story. Some will have to do with misinterpretations based on other stories used as a framework for building this one. Some will have to do with lack of skills or resources to make sense of the data. Some might have to do with people's hesitancy to put themselves on the line and commit to a conclusion. Some may have to do with worry about progressing on into the next part of the cycle.

Some roadblocks may be straightforward data management problems. Some will be culturally based, some may have political implications, and some will be based on a sense of priorities. Some may have to do with the personalities or self-images of the people involved. With a good guess at what's impeding the progress, you can think about how to overcome the roadblocks and become re-energized in the process. Usually, asking the people who are stuck to take a step back and to look at their own process is the best way to handle this. Sometimes diagnosis takes a little help from some-one else, a counselor or facilitator, who can make some quick in-terventions to help the process.

Organizations that do the best jobs in organizational learning do the following things well:

- Have infrastructure, processes, and practices for mov-ing information across the organization's boundaries

- Habitually disseminate and integrate new information into the organization's collective knowledge base and practices

- Practice collective interpretation of information, foster mutual learning, and take advantage of diverse perspec-tives for optimum analysis, understanding, and follow-up

- Exploit opportunities for innovation and change

- Impart local authority to act responsibly on valid new information

- Measure results and capture lessons learned

- Regularly debrief operations or incidents openly and candidly to discover new information and guide future actions

- Openly and candidly discuss present realities, intentions, capabilities, and any gaps that exist

- Use information to understand and improve, rather than to assign blame and apply punishment

Developing Ongoing Capability to Support Organizational Learning

After designing your process thread, you will have to consider the same elements as in the previous tasks on implementation planning and managing the transition. The organizational capability to support organizational learning is required to enable the process. Going through a large-scale change builds a foundation for this capability. The next step is to begin applying the knowledge on a continual basis. Continuous process improvement, as an enabler of change, is always about high performance for the organization. We have found the key enabler of process improvement to be applying the learning cycle as a technology for change.

The Learning Cycle As a Technology for Change

The learning cycle not only provides a diagnostic tool and guidance for helping facilitate the learning process, but it also provides a technology for steering change. Seen in this light, it is often referred to as "action research." We show it as the preferred approach in the upper-right pane of the Change Window in Chapter Two (see Figure 2.3). Action research is a process for people doing research on themselves. They are both research designers and subjects of the "experiment," both analysts of the outcomes and learners of the messages contained in them. The process of action research, illustrated in Figure 10.2, is explicit, planned, and follows the processes of the learning cycle.

An action cycle will take you twice around the learning cycle. It begins in quadrant 2, with data collection about an organizational event or characteristic that is of interest. These attention grabbers could be from the findings in Task I, the dialogues in Task II, the analyses in Task V, the difficulties of progressing that we talked about in this chapter, or wherever. The people, who are their own subjects, come together to make a joint analysis of the situation from the data and generalize about what is causing the situation. As we commented in an earlier chapter, this can be a sensitive process because the microscope has been replaced by a mirror when one is doing research on oneself. Once the people have made their joint diagnosis, they plan collaborative action—an "intervention" in their system. From the intervention they gather data, analyze what happened, and generalize about why. In the double cycle they learn about themselves, their system, and better ways to go after what they want. A flow of these action research cycles, some short loops, some very long in duration, moves the organization another step toward its change goals. We aren't trying to make this sound simple

Figure 10.2. Action Research.

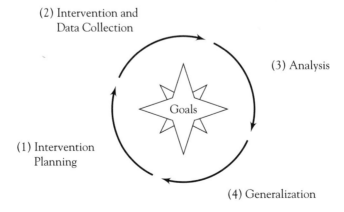

(2) Intervention and
Data Collection

(3) Analysis

Goals

(1) Intervention
Planning

(4) Generalization

or unique. This is the basic rhythm of the field of organization development, with an expansive base of theory and practice, extensive literature, and thousands of practitioners. There are other theory bases and approaches for influencing organization change (Bennis, Benne, & Chin, 1969). This learning approach forms one of the strong foundations of our field.

Planning for Closure and Celebration

A final piece of work in the Ten Tasks is to take a long, slow backward look at the journey you have taken and plan for closure and celebration. There are many people who will have dedicated great amounts of time and effort to the cause, often at great personal sacrifice, who now will move on from this piece of work to the next. There will be teams that need time to close down and finish their work before moving on. There are transitional structures in the organization that will be operating for some time in the future, then disappearing. All of these must be attended to in terms of planning when they will stop and supporting that process in a way that honors their hard work.

Now is the time to go back through the work and structures of the earlier tasks and review what will happen to them now. Three key questions to ask for each of the structures and teams that were created during the process are:

1. Is their work complete?

2. Is any of the transitional work moving into a work unit on a permanent basis? If so, have the people had adequate time to prepare the handoff?

3. Have the people involved had adequate time to close down their work, say goodbye to their teammates, and plan ahead for the next piece of work?

Review each structure and team that was created and ensure that these questions have been addressed. While it may not seem to do much for the change you have just finished, it will work won-ders for making the next change easier. If you recall, in Task I, one of the change readiness questions relates to people's past experience with change. The time spent here is an investment in building pos-itive experiences.

Last, take one more tour through the communication networks of the organization. When you started, you were dialoguing about the future—the change that was about to occur. This time, dialogue about what happened and what people learned about themselves. Deal with the feelings related to the effort now, rather than at the start of the next change. Honor and respect the effort people have committed to this change, recognize that there will always be more work to do and other changes to come, and move into the future you have collectively created.

Summary

During this task, you have done both the work of closure for the structures and teams created during the Ten Tasks and the future-focused work of creating a greater degree of change readiness for the future. The work of this task has great potential to impact your or-ganization's success. One of the reasons we have seen that organi-zations have slow learning processes is that the required learning integration activities are outside of the scope of any jobs. By creat-ing learning processes that are spread throughout the organization and are required of everyone, you build the capacity to adapt rapidly into the organization.

Points to Remember

Change Stewardship Is Guiding Collaborative Action. The work is to guide and support the learning process, ensuring that the right peo-ple are in the room and are collaborating on all parts of the learn-ing cycle.

Organization Change Stalls When the Learning Cycle Is Blocked or Interrupted and Accelerates When It Is Followed Fully. Pay attention to how the organization moves around the cycle from one quadrant to another. Encourage the people to understand and use the rhythm of the cycle, and help them work their way through any sticking points.

Dedicate the Time to Closure and Finishing. Pay attention to what processes must close down, which have to transition, and which will continue into the future. Support people with the resources and time required to do the work.

Common Trip Points

Treating the Learnings from Change as Codifiable Data. Knowledge management systems capture lessons learned in codifiable form. People hold learnings in many forms. Recognize that many of the learnings from the change are held in people's hearts and minds and can only be tapped through engagement and dialogue. Their learnings will only be explicit in their new actions.

Stopping the Engagement Structures Required for the Change. The engagement structures from the first few tasks will have to continue to operate for some time, at least through processing the results and impacts of the change.

11

A Checklist

You have now worked your way through all ten tasks. This closing chapter summarizes the information you have encountered. We have written it as a standalone checklist to be used as a pocket guide to assess where you are in a change effort and to discuss the requirements of the project with others. The relevance of each item and how much attention you must pay to it specifically will depend on the nature of your change situation, the magnitude of the changes involved, and how collaboratively (employee involved) the change work is. For example, on the technical side of things, the more process boundaries that will be crossed, the larger the impact on collateral systems, and the deeper the skills and knowledge change required, the more specific attention you will have to pay to the work of the Ten Tasks. On the organizational side of things, the greater the number of hierarchical boundaries crossed, the greater the number and diversity of functions involved, and the deeper the cultural change required, the more specific attention you will have to pay to the work of the Ten Tasks.

The Ten Tasks and the items listed under each are not a cookbook, but they will help you keep your priorities straight. In the first four tasks listed, the five items highlighted with italic type are particularly important to address carefully and thoughtfully—no matter the order of magnitude of the change you face.

As you read through the checklist, keep the following points—the beliefs about change that guide our work—in mind.

- People change because they choose to change.

- The overarching goal of any organization change is constant: high performance.

- An organization is a work system, so for change to take hold it has to address all the elements.

- Implementation of change begins with the first encounter.

- Successful change is an informed, open process.

- Change leadership is guiding collaborative action learning.

- For change to last, it has to optimize business, process, and human requirements jointly.

The Checklist

Task 1: Appreciating the Situation

- Understand your organization's environment, the alignment of your purpose or "mission" in relation to it, and your present and historical performance.

- Examine the state of your organization's major processes and practices and prioritize problems and gaps.

- Estimate the scope and impact of the changes needed to fix misalignments, address problems, and close the gaps.

- Judge the organization's readiness for and past experience with these kinds of change.

- Estimate the magnitude of the change stewardship work to move ahead.

- *Define the potential benefits and costs of changing and preparing a compelling business-based case for change.*

Task II: Developing Strategic Alignment

- Develop a communication strategy and establish a robust communication network.

- Develop a dialogue about the state of the business and the major processes.

- Develop a dialogue about the case for change.

- Learn about alternatives.

- *Develop a compelling vision for the future.*

- Develop a strategy and proposed approach to changing.

- Develop a high-level action plan.

- Implement an infrastructure to manage the process.

Task III: Evoking Change Leadership

- Establish a leadership network.

- *Involve potential change leaders in exploring "local visions" that support the overall vision for the future.*

- Enable the leadership network to act.

- Define change leadership behaviors for "walking the talk."

- Provide support for preparing for the following future roles:

    Education in potential new roles and role requirements
    Career planning

Facilitation for managing personal change

- Clearly define the leadership rewards and consequences.

- Identify and secure the required support and resources for the work ahead.

Task IV: Expanding Understanding and Commitment

- Establish "safety nets" for the organization.

- Establish role structures for the change process.

- *Establish widespread understanding of the change.*

- Begin appropriate education processes for the entire organization.

- *Create and support ongoing dialogue for the change process.*

- Use feedback systems.

- Create a more detailed action plan.

Task V: Analyzing Processes

- Clarify the work system's purpose and boundaries.

- Understand the core, value-adding transformation process of the organization.

- Understand the work system outcomes and the customers of them.

  Focus on the required outcomes of what people do, rather than on their tasks.

  Define variances that must be kept in control for successful operations.

  Identify information, work, and technologies required to manage the process and control the variances.

- Understand the impact of present organizational structures, boundaries, and processes.

    Explore the enhancing or detracting effects relative to controlling the technical processes, dealing with the environment, and adapting to the future.

    Explore the enhancing or detracting effects on the quality of work life of the members.

- Analyze support systems requirements.

    Explore how well support systems are oriented toward supporting the core transformation processes and the required changes.

- Understand the impact of present organizational structures, boundaries, and processes.

- Specify work system capability requirements.

Task VI: Designing Processes, Work, and Boundaries

- Jointly optimize the work system requirements: business needs, enhanced work system performance, and quality of work life.

- Keep a strong focus on increasing effectiveness and flexibility in controlling processes and dealing with the environment, not just on designing structure, "having teams," or implementing a flashy initiative.

- Assure that the "end product" requirements and the sources of variance during the transformation process are well understood.

- Locate boundaries in ways that enhance sharing information, process variance control, contingency management, and learning.

- Assure that the output requirements of work units are

formalized and well understood by the people, that their impact on the end product is clear, and that the work units will have access to their customers for feedback.

- Assure that the people, work units, and organizations have or can acquire the repertoire of skills and abilities necessary to manage the process within their boundaries, handle contingencies, and deal effectively with their environment.

- Assure that people who require resources to carry out responsibilities will have access and authority to use them.

- Clarify the organization structure.

- Document a provisional design.

Task VII: Planning Implementation

- Validate the design against the following elements:

  Mission, core values, and vision.
  Stakeholders' wants and expectations.
  Ability to control your variances.
  Quality-of-work-life values.

- Identify further design work.

- Establish timelines for design work.

- Establish transition management process.

- Establish integration processes and issue-resolution forums.

- Identify individuals or teams to complete the remaining work.

Task VIII: Establishing Metrics

- Determine the focus of the assessment system

  Where will the information go and who will use it?
  How is it to be used and for what purposes?

- Identify the organization's learning need from the system.

- Identify the organization's levels of output.

- Identify the categories of performance.

- Identify the realistic metrics for categories.

- Reinforce appropriate behavior.

- Set the scope of the assessment system.

- Determine the methods for data collection and analysis.

- Determine format, feedback, and evaluation processes.

- Agree on level of standardization.

- Establish linkage to reward system.

Task IX: Managing Transitions

- Maintain constancy of purpose and positive strategic intent.

  Assure that objectives remain strategy-driven.

  Assure your strategic intent is well understood and remains well aligned with the environment.

  Assure the strategy remains future-oriented.

  Assure the strategy continues to reflect a *joint* optimization of business, operating, and human values.

  Assure the environment, purpose, values, processes,

and product are well understood both "globally" and
"locally."

Assure that *all* people affected *really* understand the
nature and the implications of the change.

- Define work-unit skills, knowledge, and leadership requirements and plan the distribution among the roles.

- Establish decision slopes with each work unit, and plan
the requirements and pacing of the transitions.

- Plan and support the development of individual
abilities.

Task X: Continuous Learning and Improvement

- Understand your organizational learning process.

- Design your organizational learning process thread.

- Develop ongoing capability to support organizational
learning.

- Plan for closure and celebration.

The importance of Task X is underscored by the fact that *the beginning of work-system analysis and design is* the start of implementation, and the start of implementation is the beginning of redesign.
With the process of analysis and design comes deeper understanding and the beginning of change. With implementation comes evaluation, learning, and drivers for continuing adaptation. This is
essential for effective continuous improvement. In other words, Task
X really begins in Task I. The process for accomplishing the Ten
Tasks should be guided by the thoughtful application of principles
and practices for effective organizational learning, adaptation, continuous improvement, mastery, and renewal.

References

Ackoff, R.L. (1994). Systems thinking and thinking systems. *System Dynamics Review, 10*(2–3), 175–188.

Argyris, C.A., & Schön, D.A. (1996). *Organizational learning II: Theory, methods, and practice.* Reading, MA: Addison-Wesley.

Beckhard, R. (1978). Strategies for large systems change. In W.A. Pasmore & J.J. Sherwood (Eds.), *Sociotechnical systems: A sourcebook.* San Francisco, CA: Jossey-Bass/Pfeiffer.

Beckhard, R., & Harris, R. (1987). *Organizational transitions* (2nd ed.). Reading, MA: Addison-Wesley.

Bennis, W.G., Benne, K.D., & Chin, R. (Eds.). (1969). *The planning of change.* New York: Holt, Rinehart & Winston.

Bion, W.R. (1961). *Experiences in groups and other papers.* New York: Basic Books.

Block, P. (1993). *Stewardship: Choosing service over self-interest.* San Francisco, CA: Berrett-Koehler.

Brown, S.L., & Eisenhardt, K.M. (1997). The art of continuous change: Linking complexity theory and time-paced evolution in relentlessly shifting organizations. *Administrative Science Quarterly, 42*(3), 1–34.

Bunker, B.B., & Alban, B.T. (1997). *Large group interventions.* San Francisco, CA: Jossey-Bass.

Cherns, A. (1976). Principles of sociotechnical design revisited. *Human Relations, 40*(3), 153–162.

Christensen, T.D. (1991). *The STS design handbook.* South Bend, IN: STS Publishing.

Clegg, M. (2000). *Planning a communications and engagement strategy.* Unpublished manuscript.

Deming, W.E. (1986). *Out of the crisis*. Cambridge, MA: Massachusetts Institute of Technology, Center for Advanced Engineering Study.

Emery, F.E. (Ed.). (1969). *Systems thinking*. Middlesex, England, UK: Penguin Books.

Emery, F.E., & Emery, M. (1993). Participative design. In M. Emery (Ed.), *Participative design for participative democracy*. Caberra, ACT: Centre for Continuing Education, Australian National University.

Emery, F.E., & Trist, E.L. (1973). *Towards a social ecology*. New York: Plenum.

Emery, F.E., & Trist, E.L. (1978). Analytical model for socio-technical systems. In W.A. Pasmore & J.J. Sherwood (Eds.), *Sociotechnical systems: A sourcebook*. San Francisco, CA: Jossey-Bass/Pfeiffer.

Evans, M.J., & Thach, E. (2000). Towards the next generation change model. *OD Practitioner, 32*(4).

Festinger, L. (1957). *A theory of cognitive dissonance*. Stanford, CA: Stanford University Press.

Festinger, L. (1964). *Conflict, decisions, and dissonance*. Stanford, CA: Stanford University Press.

Galbraith, J. (1977). *Organization design*. Reading, MA: Addison-Wesley.

Galbraith, J. (1982, Winter). Designing the innovating organization. *Organizational Dynamics*, pp. 5–25.

Galbraith, J. (1994). *Competing with flexible lateral organizations*. Reading, MA: Addison-Wesley.

Garfield, C.A. (1984). *Peak performance*. New York: Warner Books.

Hanna, D.P. (1988). *Designing organizations for high performance*. Reading, MA: Addison-Wesley.

Herzberg, F. (1976). *The managerial choice: To be efficient and to be human*. Homewood, IL: Dow Jones-Irwin.

Holman, P., & Devane, T. (Eds.). (1999). *The change handbook: Group methods for shaping the future*. San Francisco, CA: Berrett-Koehler.

Jacobs, R.W. (1994). *Real time strategic change*. San Francisco, CA: Berrett-Koehler.

Jayaram, G.K. (1976). Open systems planning. In W.G. Bennis, K.D. Benne, R. Chin, & K. Corey (Eds.), *The planning of change* (3rd ed.) (pp. 275–283). New York: Holt, Rinehart & Winston.

Kaplan, R.S. (1994, September/October). Devising a balanced scorecard matched to business strategy. *Planning Review, 22*(5), 15.

Kaplan, R.S., & Norton, D.P. (1992, January/February). The balanced scorecard—Measures that drive performance. *Harvard Business Review, 70*(1), 71.

Kaplan, R.S., & Norton, D.P. (1996, January/February). Using the balanced scorecard as a strategic management system. *Harvard Business Review, 74*(1), 75.

Katz, D., & Kahn, R.L. (1978). *The social psychology of organizations*. New York: John Wiley & Sons.

Katz, D., & Kahn, R.L. (1990). *The social psychology of organizations* (Vol. II). New York: John Wiley & Sons.

Kolb, D. (1976). *The learning style inventory: Technical manual*. Boston, MA: McBer.

Lakein, A. (1973). *How to get control of your life and time*. New York: Signet.

Lewin, K. (1947). Frontiers in group dynamics, part 1: Concept, method and reality in social science: Social equilibria and social change. *Human Relations, 1*, 5–41.

Lewin, K. (1951). *Field theory in social science*. New York: Harper & Row.

Lewin, K., Lippitt, R., & White, R.K. (1939). Patterns of aggressive behavior in experimentally created social climates. *Journal of Social Psychology, 10*, 271–299.

Lytle, W.O. (1998). *Designing a high-performance organization*. Clark, NJ: Block, Petrella and Weisbord.

Maurer, R. (1996). *Beyond the wall of resistance*. Austin, TX: Bard Books.

Miller, G. (1982, September). Managing change in a changing environment. *Journal of Training and Development.*

Miller, G. (1999). The leadership dimension. In E. Biech (Ed.), *The 1999 annual: Vol. 1, training*. San Francisco, CA: Jossey-Bass/Pfeiffer.

Nadler, D.A. (1998). *Champions of change*. San Francisco, CA: Jossey-Bass.

Nadler, D.A., Gerstein, M.C., & Shaw, R.B. (1992). *Organizational architecture*. San Francisco, CA: Jossey-Bass.

Nevis, E.C. (1987). *Organizational consulting: A gestalt approach*. Cleveland, OH: Gestalt Institute of Cleveland Press.

Nevis, E.C., Lancourt, J., & Vassallo, H.G. (1996). *Intentional revolutions*. San Francisco, CA: Jossey-Bass.

Owen, H. (1997). *Open space technology: A user's guide*. San Francisco, CA: Berrett-Koehler.

Pasmore, W.A., & Sherwood, J.J. (1978). *Sociotechnical systems: A sourcebook*. San Francisco, CA: Jossey-Bass/Pfeiffer.

Pava, C. (1984). *Managing new office technology: An organizational strategy*. New York: The Free Press.

Peters, T.J., & Waterman, R.H. (1982). *In search of excellence*. New York: Harper & Row.

Pfeiffer, J.W., & Jones, J.E. (1980). *User's guide to the structured experience kit.* San Francisco, CA: Jossey-Bass/Pfeiffer.

Rogers, E.M. (1995). *Diffusion of innovations* (4th ed.). New York: The Free Press.

Rokeach, M. (1970). *Beliefs, attitudes, and values.* San Francisco, CA: Jossey-Bass.

Rothwell, W.J. (1999). *The action learning guidebook.* San Francisco, CA: Jossey-Bass/Pfeiffer.

Schein, E.H. (1985). *Organizational culture and leadership.* San Francisco, CA: Jossey-Bass.

Senge, P.M. (1990). *The fifth discipline: The art and practice of the learning organization.* New York: Doubleday Currency.

Senge, P.M., Kleiner, A., Roberts, C., Ross, R., & Smith, B. (1994). *The fifth discipline fieldbook: Strategies and tools for building a learning organization.* New York: Bantam Doubleday Dell.

Storm, H. (1972). *Seven arrows.* New York: Ballantine.

Taylor, J.C., & Felten, D.F. (1993). *Performance by design: Sociotechnical systems in North America.* Englewood Cliffs, NJ: Prentice Hall.

Trist, E., Emery, F., & Murray, H. (Eds.). (1993). *The social engagement of social science volume II: The socio-technical perspective.* Philadelphia, PA: University of Pennsylvania Press.

von Bertalanffy, L. (1968). *General systems theory.* New York: George Braziller.

Weber, M. (1947). *The theory of social and economic organization.* New York: The Free Press.

Weisbord, M.R. (1987). *Productive workplaces: Organizing and managing for dignity, meaning, and community.* San Francisco, CA: Jossey-Bass.

Weisbord, M., & Janov, S. (1995). *Future search: An action guide to finding common ground for organizations and communities.* San Francisco, CA: Berrett-Koehler.

Wheatley, M.J. (1994). *Leadership and the new science.* San Francisco, CA: Berrett-Koehler.

Wheatley, M.J., & Kellner-Rogers, M. (1996). *A simpler way.* San Francisco, CA: Berrett-Koehler.

Wilbur, K. (1996). *A brief history of everything.* London, England: Shambhala.

About the Authors

Jeff Evans practices in the area of human systems and organizational capability. His early work years were spent in retail and manufacturing, where he experienced the work of both change agent and change target. He has since worked as both an internal and external organization development practitioner. In the past few years, his work has included both new and redesigned manufacturing organizations and company-level redesigns, both domestic and international. These designs incorporated current practices in high-performance organizations and the principles of the learning organization. He has undergraduate and graduate degrees in education and social sciences and human resource development from Lamar University and Texas A&M. In graduate school, he specialized in organization development and instructional system design. He has done post-doctoral work in behavioral systems, organizations, and the psychology of group dynamics. He is a graduate of the three-year post-graduate track at the Gestalt Institute of Cleveland and teaches at the University of California Berkeley Extension in human resource development.

Chuck Schaefer is an experienced professional in the field of organization development and design. He has spent about a third of his professional career as a systems architect and program manager in advanced aerospace systems, a third as an external organization development and design consultant, and a third as an internal organization consultant in a variety of organizational settings. He has also held university faculty appointments in organization, management, organization development, experiential education, and human psychology. His undergraduate studies were in aerospace engineering at the University of Illinois, and his advanced graduate work was in applied behavioral science, open systems, high-performance organization, and humanistic psychology at the University of California, Los Angeles. He holds special certification in neuro-linguistics programming, applied guided imagery, small-group development, and experiential education. In the past few years, he has spent most of his time supporting major organization change and leadership development in relation to high-performance work systems and major business process reinvention.

Index